HowE Guide t Dancıng

101+ Tips to Learn How to Belly Dance from A to Z

HowExpert with Aneta Dimoska

For more tips related to this topic, visit HowExpert.com/bellydancing.

Recommended Resources

- HowExpert.com – Quick 'How To' Guides on All Topics from A to Z by Everyday Experts.
- HowExpert.com/free – Free HowExpert Email Newsletter.
- HowExpert.com/books – HowExpert Books
- HowExpert.com/courses – HowExpert Courses
- HowExpert.com/clothing – HowExpert Clothing
- HowExpert.com/membership – HowExpert Membership Site
- HowExpert.com/affiliates – HowExpert Affiliate Program
- HowExpert.com/writers – Write About Your #1 Passion/Knowledge/Expertise & Become a HowExpert Author.
- HowExpert.com/resources – Additional HowExpert Recommended Resources
- YouTube.com/HowExpert – Subscribe to HowExpert YouTube.
- Instagram.com/HowExpert – Follow HowExpert on Instagram.
- Facebook.com/HowExpert – Follow HowExpert on Facebook.

Publisher's Foreword

Dear HowExpert Reader,

HowExpert publishes quick 'how to' guides on all topics from A to Z by everyday experts.

At HowExpert, our mission is to discover, empower, and maximize talents of everyday people to ultimately make a positive impact in the world for all topics from A to Z...one everyday expert at a time!

All of our HowExpert guides are written by everyday people just like you and me who have a passion, knowledge, and expertise for a specific topic.

We take great pride in selecting everyday experts who have a passion, great writing skills, and knowledge about a topic that they love to be able to teach you about the topic you are also passionate about and eager to learn about.

We hope you get a lot of value from our HowExpert guides and it can make a positive impact in your life in some kind of way. All of our readers including you altogether help us continue living our mission of making a positive impact in the world for all spheres of influences from A to Z.

If you enjoyed one of our HowExpert guides, then please take a moment to send us your feedback from wherever you got this book.

Thank you and we wish you all the best in all aspects of life.

Sincerely,

BJ Min
Founder & Publisher of HowExpert
HowExpert.com

PS...If you are also interested in becoming a HowExpert author, then please visit our website at HowExpert.com/writers. Thank you & again, all the best!

Table of Contents

Chapter 1: Before We Start

I have a belief that everyone carries a unique story, a story that comes from deep within, a story that reveals our soul and speaks from our inner emotions. Well, that story, my dear friends, is worth to be shared. Therefore, here is mine.

Going back into the 2000s, I still remember the time when I was watching TV, and it started occupying most of my free time. What I have found most interesting about the new movie was the presented culture and how it differed from any other film I had seen before. I was a young teenage girl, and besides the fact that the unconditional love between the actors touched me, there was something deeper that caught my attention. It was belly dancing. The plot of the movie took part in Morocco, and the scenes abounded with Middle East music, dance, culture, costumes.

I was fascinated by the energy, the smoothness that was presented by the women who danced, and at that moment, I felt that this music was awakening some new part within me. I knew that sooner this is going to become a way to express my feelings, a little escape from reality, offering me a comfortable space to grow my spirit. And yes, I wasn't wrong. Very soon, I started turning cloths into props that were used for my first choreographies in front of the mirror, without anyone watching, of course.

The excitement of the unknown was flourishing. It was causing me to become curious and want to explore and dig into the movements and positions of the body. At that time, my steps were improvisations of something that probably does not exist in belly dance, ...but to be honest, I did not care. I was putting on the clothes (some skirts and dresses from my mom), turning on the music....and action!

It took a while before I realize that belly dancing will become my oasis in the middle of the desert. As the years were passing by, I was not investing professionally to improve this dance, but I was following other dancers and learning from their techniques. A set of circumstances have led to this situation, but after some time, I had no choice but to ask belly dancing for help. It was a challenging period on an emotional level for me where I was at a point where I wanted to find what, deeply, and truly fulfilled me to pass through the period more painlessly. Once again, I was very open to myself and confessed that maybe now it is the best time to explore this dance and to allow myself to take on this journey.

Ever since the first class, I have felt that I have found the missing piece all these years. Since the first class, belly dancing has become the time to boost my self-discovery, self-esteem, and energy. It is my recovery and relief, my space for creativity and imagination.

In the following chapters, I hope that I will grab your attention and take you to this beautiful journey. All you need is an open mind and heart for new adventures, some space to allow the movements, a source of music, and a piece of positive energy. Enjoy!

Warm-Up Exercises

In this part, I would like to underline the importance of practicing warm-up exercises before starting with the dance. Dance requires movements with all components and muscles of your body, and if not warmed up enough, you could end up with a bad stretch or burning in your muscles.

Please do not skip this routine and instead make it your ritual before you start. It will only take 5 – 10 minutes.

You can be very creative when it comes to warming up exercise because they will give you a beautiful set up for the steps that follow.

Start by warming up your upper part of the body, head, and shoulders. Stretch the waist and the stomach muscles. Pay attention to the hips and legs, and do not forget the feet and toes.

Belly Dance Posture

Every belly dancing movement requires having the right body posture.

Why belly dance posture matters?

Preparing the body. By having the correct belly dance posture, we prepare the body for the coming movements, and it makes easier the transition from one to another step.

Improving multitasking. We continuously have to be aware of our bodies and pay attention to the moves that sometimes can be struggling. It may be a bit challenging to pay attention to the choreography, the music, and the space around you or the audience in the beginning. However, this technique allows you to become more comfortable and self-confident.

Balance. One of the most important things to develop in belly dancing is the BALANCE. Find the balance for the best position. Find the balance to stand on the ball of the toes. Find the balance when you shift the weight from one leg to another.

Like many other parts in belly dancing, balance takes time to improve, so let's start finding the primary balance on the toes while standing in the basic belly dance posture. Here are some tips:

Feet

Tip #1 – Find a balance

Start by standing on your feet slightly opened just underneath your hipbones. Bend your knees very slightly, and **find a balance point** on the ground to stand on.

Try to **avoid leaning** on your feet balls forward or shifting the weight on your heels backward. Instead, find that point where you will be in the middle of these two positions.

Knees

Tip #2 – Keep the knees softly bent

Knees **are bent** like when you usually are walking. It should not appear as an exaggerated bending, but more like a reasonable, walking bend.

Keep the knees **soft and relaxed.**

Pelvis area

Tip #3 – Tuck the pelvis under

Having your knees bent, put your attention to the pelvis area.

The key point to understand here is to **tuck** the pelvis area under and keep the tailbone down.

Tip #4 – 'Zipping jeans' trick.

One trick that helps me to adjust my posture whenever I lose it during the dance is the following:

Imagine that you are putting on your jeans and especially pay attention to that little movement that you do with the pelvis when you **zip the jeans**.

This is what you have to remember in belly dancing. Therefore, you don't want to have a 'duck butt' looking backward, but tuck it inside, just like when you are zipping the jeans.

Also, **do not contract** the abdominal muscles too tight so that you won't have any space for further movements, but find that balance where you will feel most comfortable and natural.

Chest area

Next, move to the chest area.

Tip #5 – Lift the chest

Take the position of your chest as you usually do, inhale and slightly **lift it** above your normal position. When properly lifted, you should feel small 'burning' in your upper back muscles.

Think of your **shoulders**, lift them, roll back, drop them down, and relax. Your arms should be very smooth and relaxed too.

Arms

It would be best if you do not lift your arms too high so that you feel pain from your engagement and too low not to have any involvement.

Tip #6 - 'Office desk'

Imagine that you have an office desk in front of you and typing on the computer's keyboard. Keep that desk height in your mind and open one arm to the left and the other one to the right.

Head

Tip #7 – Lift head up

At the very end, keep your head and chin lifted enough to express your **self-esteem** and **confidence** in the performance that follows.

Basic belly dance posture

Cool-down exercises

As important as the warm-up exercises are, the cooldown section is just as necessary.

After giving your body and soul an excellent treatment while dancing, it is now time to relax and accumulate all the energy produced before.

Include mainly breathing exercises, stretching, and relaxing. You can sit down on the floor and start with gathering your breath. Again, stretch the head and neck, waist, and legs. Allow yourself to feel the benefits of the process you were in and soak the positivity that will grow even more with the next steps you take.

Review

1. Start your belly dance session by doing **warm-up** exercises. Give your body 5-10 minutes of low to medium workout, depending on your condition.
2. **Belly dance posture** is the essential starting point before you take any other step.
3. Make sure that everything on your body is **relaxed** and in the correct position.
4. Feet underneath the hips, knees soft and bent, tailbone facing down, zip the jeans and tuck in the pelvis, lift the chest, head up, chin up, arms spread out, and relaxed. Have we missed

something? Yes, a big smile on your face. Now you are in the best **belly dance posture**.

5. Do not forget to **cool down** your body after you finish dancing and exercising. Focus on stretching the muscles and relaxed and controlled breathing.

Chapter 2: Belly Dancing Hips and Lower Body Techniques

How to Do Hip Twists, Hip Slides, and Hip Lifts

One fundamental movement in belly dancing is the hip twist.

When I was starting with belly dancing, the hip twist was a move that took quite a long time to improve, mainly due to the proper isolation that is required, avoiding any movement of the upper part of the body.

Once you master the hip twist, you can do a variety of choreography, making it vivid and divine. So, take this challenge, and let's start.

Hip Twist

Belly dance posture. I am sure that by now you have understood the basic belly dance posture, so stand with the feet right under the hips, knees are soft and bent, pelvis tucked in, the chest lifted, head up, and arms spread and opened out.

Tip #8 - 'The Clock'

Imagine that you are standing in the center of a clock. In front of you is 12, your right hip points to 3 o'clock, your back is on six, and the left hip is pointing to nine.

What we want to achieve is to bring each hip from its neutral position to 12.

As you are standing in the basic posture,

- Start moving the **left hip forward**, taking it from nine, and bringing it to 12. It will look like you are doing a small arc with the hip.
- You have noticed that as you move the hip forward, the **right hip is going backward** and moving from 3 to 6 o'clock. This result is coming very naturally because, otherwise, the right hip cannot stay stationary and has to go back to allow the left hip to twist.
- Now, bring the **left hip to the center** and try with the opposite side.
- Take the right hip out of the neutral position (3 o'clock) and **bring it forward to** 12. As you notice, this time, the left hip is going back to six.
- Now, let's connect each twist of the hip so that you see a **fluid movement**. The goal is to merge both hip twists as a whole, skipping any pausing in between.

Hip Twist

1. Left hip twists forwards

2. Right hip twists forwards

Turn on some belly dance music and start very, but very slowly to twist one hip at a time and then the other.

The hips are moving very coordinated because when the hip is forward, the opposite is going back and prepares to come forward so that the other one can go back.

What is the rest of the body doing while twisting?

- Knees are soft and slightly bent; do not forget to breathe, and as you feel comfortable, increase the pace and do the twist even faster and faster (as much as you can).

Tip #9 – Keep it horizontal

This movement is **only horizontal**, which is why it is crucial to have the upper part of the body stationary and stable.

One thing to remember here is the stillness of the knees while twisting.

Whenever you make the twist to the front, make sure that the knee stays stable and still should not be moving forward with the hip. Even when you twist faster, the knees have to be stationary all the time.

Benefits from the hip twist. This technique, besides giving you a bunch of opportunities to make your choreography outstanding and diverse it will also give you a very nicely shaped waist.

Stand again in the basic posture and place both of your palms on the middle abs' muscles. While you make the twist with the left hip, press the palm in the belly to feel the engagement in the right side muscles. Again, twist the right hip to the front and feel the burning now in the left abs muscles. Feel this engagement on both sides and enjoy the twist.

Hip Slides

Hip slides are one of the foundational movements in belly dancing. It is quite simple, fun to understand, and learn, but like many other steps, it requires time, patience, and self-control.

Tip #10 – Keep the upper part of the body stationary

During this movement, it is essential **to stay stable** with the upper body and feet and focus on hip isolation. Hip slides can have many different types of variations.

Belly dance posture. Stand with the feet right under the hips, knees are soft and slightly bent, pelvis tucked in, the chest lifted, head up, and arms spread out and relaxed.

ATTENTION: The number one thing to remember is:

- ✓ Once you have found your balance and stability, keep the body in the **center** no matter what the hips are doing.
- ✓ It means that even the hips go to the side, your upper body and shoulders will stay centered, just like your feet do.

Tip #11 – Slide the hips to the left and the right

- Start shifting your weight on the left foot and slide the left hip on the left side.
- To achieve this slide, go as far as your body allows to the left, but remember to keep your shoulders in the center all the time and then come back to the neutral position.
- Now, shift to the right and slide the right hip as far back as you can and come back to neutral.

- Every time you slide on each side, feel the engagement in the oblique muscles, which is how you will make sure that you are on the right path.
- Skip the part of coming to neutral and pausing and give your hips space and freedom to slide from one side to another.

Hip slides

For a better understanding of this movement, you can try a trick that works for me.

Tip #12 - 'The Wall' trick.

- Imagine that you are standing between two walls, just like in a narrow corridor.

- If centered, each wall is on 6-7 inches (10-15) cm distance from your hips.

- Now, imagine that you want to touch the left wall with the left hip, and then you want to do the same with the opposite hip.

- Notice that this movement from side to side is ONLY horizontal.

Tip #13 – No bouncing

Avoid any **lifting, bumping, or bouncing**. You may feel an attempt to lift each hip to the side, but instead of sliding, you end up swinging with the hips, which in this case, is not correct.

Tip #14 – No shoulder movements

Another mistake that may appear is **moving the shoulders on the opposite** side from the hips. Make sure to avoid sliding your shoulders to the right if the hips go to the left or the left if hips go to the right.

Hip slides – wrong body position

1. Avoid sliding the upper body to the opposite side of the hip

2. Avoid sliding the upper body to the opposite side of the hip

Do not be discouraged if you find yourself out of the proper position during this movement. It will happen, and it is a part of the learning process. However, you have to remember that the body and muscles need time to achieve the necessary flexibility.

After some time, these movements will become so easy to do, and you will be ready for new upgrades.

Hip lift

Hip lift is the ground for the hip locks, shimmy and many other variations.

Belly dance posture. Stand in the basic belly dance posture while your feet are underneath the hips, knees are bent, tailbone down, low abs tucked, chest lifted, head up, arms are open all the way out, and relaxed.

Tip #15 – Feet on the ground

In this movement, it is crucial to have both feet on the ground, which is very connected to the floor and stable.

In the beginning, if you feel the urge to lift one foot off the ground, you can do it, but try to focus and be aware of all parts of your body so that you have the complete control of what each part is doing.

Tip #16 – Lift the hips up and down

- While you are standing in the basic posture, **bend your knees** even more than standard. Bending your knees will allow you better isolation and floating moves with the hips.

Hip Lifts – starting position

Start by bending the
knees even more than
usual

- Start straightening the left leg (but not completely) and notice how your left hip is going up (this comes naturally because of the straightening of the leg).

- When the hip is lifting, **squeeze the oblique** muscles imagining that you want to meet the left hip with the rib cage.

Hip Lifts - left hip up

Lift the left hip, while
keeping the right knee
bent

- Then, bring back the hip **to the center** and start lifting the right hip.

- This time it will require straightening the **right leg** so that the right hip can go up and then bring it back to the center.

Hip Lifts - right hip up

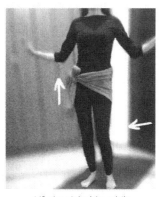

Lift the right hip, while
keeping the left knee bent

- Now, lift the left hip and see how bringing it back to the center immediately prepares the opposite leg to straighten and lift the opposite hip.

- Keep this movement connected, skipping the hold from each transition, and see how the hips move fluently and gently.

- Please have in mind that the more you try to **bend the knees** down, the easier it will be to find the isolation you need.

- Once again, this is only a hip movement, so every other bumping and bouncing with the upper body should be excluded.

Tip #17 – Do not straighten the lifting leg completely

What you want to avoid here is straightening the leg that lifts the hip. That will not give you the freedom to move the hips, but it will take you out of the basic belly dance posture very quickly as your tailbone will go up behind, and you don't want to end up with a 'duck butt.'

Hip Circles

Hip circles are fun, easy to learn, and provide you with a full palette of techniques that you can apply in belly dancing.

After you have mastered these simple techniques, you can play with them and make many improvisations. In this section, we will refer to two basic hip circles: large or exterior and small or interior.

Large hip circles

Belly dance posture. Stand with the feet right under your **shoulder width** this time, knees are soft and slightly bent, pelvis tucked in, the chest lifted, head up, and arms spread out and relaxed.

You can notice that there is more space between the feet, which will allow your pivots to be more isolated and provide your hips with enough space for circulation.

Tip #18 - **'The Cross' trick**.

We are going to use our imagination again, so let's pretend that you are standing in the middle of a cross that looks like a plus sign.

- With your left hip, try to reach the ending point of the **left part of the cross**. This movement is already familiar to you, and you recognize it as a hip slide.
- Give a big push to the left and feel the engagement in the left oblique muscles group and then bring the hip back to its neutral position.

Hip Circles - large hip circle 1/4

Reach the left point of
the 'cross'

- From the center, slide the right hip trying to meet the **right end of the cross**. You can feel the engagement in the right **oblique**, can't you?

Hip Circles - large hip circle 2/4

Reach the right point of
the 'cross'

- Bring the hip back to the neutral and now start pushing **both hips together forward** following the straight line of the cross all the way to the front. This movement will engage the upper abs, which will be an indication for a well-done job.

Push both hips forwards, reaching the front side of
the 'cross'

- As you push forward, avoid extreme leaning
  with the upper part of the body and shoulders
  backward. That is an unpleasant position and
  for sure will throw you out of what you want to
  achieve.
- Bring the hips to the neutral position and start
  pushing the **pelvis area backward**. This
  push back has to be executed with the entire
  abdominal area and the hips.

1. Push both hips backwards, reaching the back side of the 'cross'

2. Make sure that the tailbone is pointing down

Tip #19 – Be careful of leaning forward

Here you have to be cautious of two things:

- Avoid exaggerated forward leaning with the upper body.
- Make sure that when you push the hips backward, the tailbone is still facing down.

As we have reached the four main points, all you have to do is to connect them in a smooth movement to create a large circle.

Tip #20 - Create the circle

The starting point will be pushing the hips forward and with the left hip proceed to draw the circle all the way backward, stretching to the right and coming back to the neutral.

Large Hip Circles

Exterior circles are parallel with the floor. There is no up and down with the hips, but only creating parallel circles on the surface below us.

Tip #21 – Make a variation of the large circle

Make a variation of the large circle to make it more visible and dramatic.

- From the basic posture, make a small step to the side to separate the feet even more.
- Repeat the same, previous four movements (the four points of the cross), but this time with leaning the upper body to the hips' opposite directions.

- When the hips move left, the upper part of the body slides on the right, so the stretch is more dramatic. The same happens when hips go on the right side.

Variation of a large hip circle 1 /2

1. Push the left hip to the left and slide the upper body to the right

2. Push the right hip to the right and slide the upper body to the left

- When you push the hips forward, slightly lean backward with the upper body.
- On the other side, what happens when the hips go back? When the hips go backward, the upper body leans toward the front in a position bent and parallel with the floor.

Variation of a large hip circle 2/2

1. Push both hips forwards and slightly lean the upper body backwards

2. Push both hips backwards and lean with the upper body forwards - parallel to the floor

You have to perform these movements and connections very smoothly and effortlessly. They have to be so natural, soft, and feminine, expressing all the love and tenderness within you.

Variation of a large hip circle

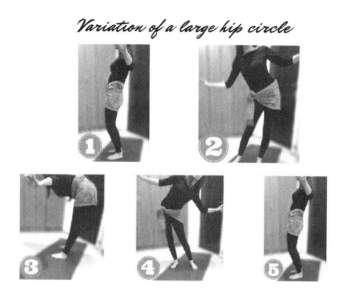

Small Hip Circles

You perform small or interior hip circles using the hip lifts, and therefore they will not be parallel to the floor.

Belly dance posture. Let's start with the standard basic belly dance posture, feet are right under the hips, knees are soft and bent, pelvis tucked in, chest lifted, head up, and arms spread out and relaxed.

Tip #22 – Make small hip circles using the hip lift technique

Engage the lower abs and tuck the pelvis even more. From this position,

- **Lift** the left hip, like as you want to meet the hip with the rib cage. (Position no. 1)

Hip circles - small hip circle 1/4

1. Lift left hip up - Position no. 1

- When the hip is going up, the **left knee** is straightening (not completely), and the right one is bending even more.
- Then softly straighten the **right knee** (not completely), and as you do so, the tailbone will naturally be pointing up instead of down. (Position no. 2)

2. Both knees slightly straighten; tailbone pointing
up - Position no. 2

- Continue by **bending** the left knee and **lifting** the right hip, meeting with the rib cage. (Position no. 3)

3. Lift right hip up and bend the left knee - Position no. 3

- End up by bending both knees and hips come to a neutral position. (Position no. 4)

4. Bend both knees and return to neutral position -
Position no. 4

- Connect these four positions into a soft, gentle circle, and practice this cycle again for faster improvements.

Hip circles - small hip circle

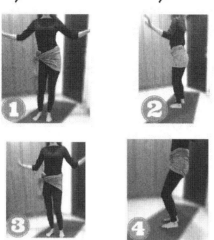

What is Opening and Closing Hip?

Belly dancing is more than just following the drum, making shimmies, or other exotic isolations with your body. It is all about the connection, the liberation, and the freedom to express your inner feelings in an elegant and sophisticated way.

Belly dancing cherishes the energy that flows in your body, both **feminine and masculine**, allowing you to express yourself in beautiful moves that come from the hips and spread all over the body.

In this section, we will focus on this division between the female and male expressions with the hips. So, do you guess which part of your body is the feminine one? – Correct, the left one.

Opening Hip

Tip #23 – Discover your left side

'Left side' meaning. The left side of the body represents the feminine traits in both women and men. It is manifested in caring and helping, expressing love and tenderness, and giving support and listening. It represents our soft side, the gentle one. It represents your feelings of being a woman, your inner and deep feminine energy, and your soul.

The hips must come first to give this 'left energy' a room to float. In the beginning, when I was watching this step in my classes, I thought: "This one is easy, I am going to smash it," but when I stood in the position, I thought: "OK, what was I thinking...teacher can you show me again?"

Don't underestimate this move at the beginning, and please do your best to try it over and over again.

How to open the hip?

Belly dance posture. Stand in the basic belly dance posture, knees bent, tailbone down, chest lifted, arms opened out and relaxed.

- Bring your left leg for about half a step forward and **open your left foot** as much as you can to the left corner. This might be a bit awkward during the first attempt, but with practice, sooner, it will become your natural position.

- Shift the weight on the left foot and notice that the left knee will ask for even more bending forward. Allow it to **bend even more**.

- Next, twist the left hip forward and bring it just above your left foot. The hip and the foot should be **parallel to each other** because they are pointing to the same left diagonal (corner).

- Now, with the left leg forward and bent knee, open your hip, stretch it and slide it as you **make a circle to the left**.

- Your left hip will point to the **left-back corner** and then bring it back to its starting position.

Tip #24 – Engage only the left hip

Remember two things:

You have to work **ONLY** with the left hip; the right hip will be moving too but only for support and

Second, keep the upper part of the body **soft and still**.

Make this movement very slowly, and be able to see the opening of your feminine energy, be gentle with your body as you are with your soul and surrounding. Express the softness you carry within you and start it over and over again.

Opening hip

Closing hip

Tip #25 – Discover your right side

'Right side' meaning. Like everything in the nature that is in a perfect balance, the same happens within the human body. Besides the feminine part, to achieve the state of equilibrium, we need the masculine part to balance.

The right side of the body represents the logic and the intellectual part of our being. It expresses rationality, assertiveness, and authority. Because this side is not so 'gentle,' in belly dance, it is used for closing movements with the hip.

How *to make the closure?*

Belly dance posture. Stand in the basic belly dance posture again and now make a small step in front of you with the right leg.

- Open the **right foot** to the right corner and slightly bend the knees.
- Shift the **weight on the left leg**; bend the left knee even more than before, and straighten the left leg accordingly.
- **Twist the right hip** backward, pointing to the right-back diagonal.
- Now push the hip to the right side (slide it on the right) and bring it to the front as you shift the weight on the right foot.
- While you are creating the circle and bringing the hip to the front, your **spine** has to be **very strong**, and your upper part of the body might lean a little bit to the front. That is normal and expected, but as long it is not exaggerated, it is allowed.

In belly dancing, almost all movement is started by engaging either the left leg or the left hip. The reason is the meaning of the energy that flows in this part of the body. Of course, we do not want to put on a pedestal left side and forget about the right one. There always has to be balanced. The balance gives you a smooth appearance in all of your performances.

Closing hip

Let's Figure 8 with Hips

Figure 8s are one of the most recognizable movements when it comes to belly dancing. Along with the other moves that we have covered so far, figure 8s are essential and put us closer to the essence of belly dancing.

Tip #26 – Expose your emotions

The main force that will drive the hips is **emotion**. You have to feel and become one with the music. Nevertheless, do not worry; this will be achieved very naturally, within time and practice.

In this section, I will guide you through *four basic groups of figure 8s*, which you can express yourself with many variations and techniques.

Until now, we have passed through the *hip lifts, drops, slides, and twists*. These are the ground for figure 8s. Figure 8s are the result of the combination of each of these hip movements.

Tip #27 - 'The Drawing' Trick

The best advice I can share with you to understand these movements quickly is to imagine that your body is a drawing tool, and your goal is to draw some imaginary figure 8s on the floor or on the wall, depending on your visualization. I highly recommend these tips because if you are a person with a visual learning style, this will help you achieve the best results faster.

Figure 8 - The Drawing trick

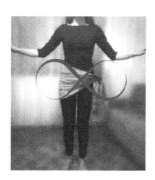 

Use your hips to draw the imaginary infinity symbol

Horizontal Figure 8

Now we are going to start with the horizontal hip movements. As the name itself indicates, these movements are going to be performed **ONLY parallel** to the floor beneath. No ups and downs, we can save them for later on.

Belly dance posture. Start with the basic belly dance posture; feet are in the width of the hips, knees are softly bent, tailbone down, lower abdominal tucked in, chest lifted, chin lifted, arms are opened and relaxed.

Tip #28 - 'The Box'

- Imagine that you are in the **center of a box**, and there are two corners in front and two in the back.

- Also, imagine that on the floor, there is the **infinity sign** ∞ (now is your time, mathematicians), and you are in the middle of this sign, just where the circles meet each other.

Imagine that you are in the center of the
infinity sign on the floor

- Furthermore, imagine that one of the circles is on your **left** and the other on your **right side**.

- Notice that **we are not** using the regular figure 8. Just for a comparison, if you are standing in the center of the standard figure 8, then one circle will be in front of you, and the other one will be behind you. This is not what we want to achieve, so do not do it.

Tip #29 - Make Horizontal Figure 8s using the hip twist and hip slide technique

Let's get back to our box and the infinity sign. While you are in the basic posture

- Start **twisting** your left hip to the front as we did in the twisting session before.

- As the hip is twisted, point it to the **left front corner** of the imaginary box,

  ✓ *Slide it* as much as you can to the left diagonal and
  ✓ Slowly start *drawing backward* the left circle of the sign ∞.

- Now the left hip points to the **left back corner** of the box, while the right hip is twisted and ready for drawing.

Horizontal Figure 8 - hip twist and hip slide 1/2

1. Twist and slide the left hip forwards to the left front corner

2. Slide left hip to the left side

3. Twist left hip backwards to the left back corner

- Remember, that while you draw the circle, your **chest** does not come along with the hip backward.

- The chest is faced to the front and is **stationary** all the time. I know that you may find it an uncomfortable position for the body. You will start dancing correctly as soon as you get the flexibility, especially in the oblique muscles.

- Put your attention on the right hip as it points towards the **right front diagonal** (corner) of the box.

- **Slide the hip** towards that direction (front right corner) and again draw the right circle of the infinity sign with the hip as it moves slowly **backward**.

Horizontal Figure 8 - hip twist and hip slide 2/2

4. Right hip is now twisted and slide to the right front corner

5. Slide right hip to the right side

6. Twist the right hip backwards to the right back corner

- Now, **try it again** with the left hip going front, slide to the diagonal, bring it back as it draws the circle, and repeat the same with the right hip.

- Notice that as the hip slides to one side, the **body's weight** is shifted to the same side.

- Increase the speed at the moment when you feel more comfortable.

- **Congratulations**, you have succeeded in the first figure 8.

- This type of figure 8 is the first of the four groups of 8s and is called **Horizontal figure 8 front and back or Egyptian figure 8s.**

Tip #30 - Reverse figure 8 or Turkish figure 8s

As you are already guessing, the second group will be the opposite of the first one: **Horizontal figure 8 back and front (reverse figure 8 or Turkish figure 8s).**

- Now start with the left hip twisting it to the **left back** corner of the box.

- **Slide it** gently to this direction (left back corner) and from there,

- Start **drawing** the left **circle** all the way to the front.

1. Twist and slide left hip to the left back corner

2. Slide left hip to the left side

3. End up with twisting the left hip to the left front corner

- When the left hip has come to the front, the right hip has expectedly twisted backward to point on the **right back corner** of the box.

- Push the right hip towards this diagonal (right back corner), and as it slides, start **drawing** the right **circle** up to the front.

4. Right hip is now twisted to the right back corner

5. Slide right hip to the right side

6. Bring the right hip to the right front corner

- Try it again with the left hip: twist to the back, slide to the corner, bring it to the front, and continue with the right hip.

Have fun while you are exploring these movements, turn on belly dancing music, and enjoy the process.

I hope that you have understood the differences between these two types of figure 8s that are performed with the hips parallel to the floor.

There was no lifting or dropping hip simply because that is another group of figure 8s: Vertical figure 8s.

Vertical Figure 8s

One of my favorites and the most feminine movements in belly dancing are vertical figure 8s. These are sensual isolations that enrich the choreography, especially when the music is low paced and when emotions are needed to unveil the story behind the music.

Opposite of the horizontal, vertical 8s are not parallel to the floor, requiring coordination of different hip positions.

Belly dance posture. We are going to start with the basic belly dance posture: feet are in the width of the hips, knees softly bent, tailbone down, lower abdominal tucked in, chest lifted, chin lifted, and arms are open and relaxed.

Tip # 31 – Make vertical figure 8s using the hip lift and hip slide

- Imagine that the infinity sign is in front of you in the **height** of your lower abs (pelvis).

- Also, imagine that your **belly button is a pencil,** and you want to draw the infinity sign in front of you ∞.

Vertical Figure 8

Imagine the infinity sign in front of your hips

- **Bend the knees** even more than usual,

- **Lift** the left hip, and as it lifts, start sliding it to the left, following the line of the left infinity sign circle.

- As you draw the line, the hip slowly drops down.

Vertical Figure 8 – hip lift and hip slide 1/2

1. Lift left hip up

2. Slide left hip to the left side

3. Drop left hip down

- Remember that when you slide the hip to the left, you have to **push it**, stretching the left oblique muscles as much as your body allows.

What is happening with the knees?

- As the left hip lifts, left knee is straightening (but not wholly), and as the hip slides and drops down, the knee is coming to the first (bent) position allowing the right knee to start straightening and preparing the right hip to lift.

Now, you should have the **right hip lifted** and ready to draw the right line of our imaginary sign with the navel pencil.

- It will initiate slowly sliding on the right side and dropping the hip down.
- The right knee bends, allows the left knee to straighten, and starts the cycle again from the beginning.

Vertical Figure 8 - hip lift and hip slide 2/2

4. As left hip drops down, right hip lifts up

5. Slide right hip to the right side

6. Drop right hip down

- Try it again with lifting the hip, sliding to the side, slowly dropping, then lift the opposite hip and repeat the same movement. This type of vertical figure 8s is known as **Maya or Vertical figure 8s up and down**.

Tip #32 – Reverse the direction of the Vertical figure 8s

There is one more type of vertical figure 8s that is reverse to the Mayas: **Egyptian vertical figure 8s down and up**.

- Get back in the basic belly dance posture, keep in your mind the infinity sign in front of you.

- Bend the knees more than usual so that you have better **isolation** and start with the left hip drop.

- That will result in bending the left knee and slightly straightening of the right knee.

- As you drop your hips, **stretch it** to the left and **lift it** while you draw the left side of the circle.

- You will end up with the left hip up and with a softly straightened left knee.

Reverse Vertical Figure 8 - 1/2

1. Drop left hip down

2. Lift and slide left hip to the left side

3. Lift left hip up

- Keep the left hip up, as if it wants to meet the rib cage, squeezing the oblique muscles.

- In this position, the right knee bends more than before, preparing the right hip to start sliding on the side and slowly lifting.

Reverse Vertical Figure 8 - 2/2

4. As left hip lifts up, right hip drops down

5. Lift and slide right hip to the right side

6. Lift right hip up

- Try it again slowly, and as you feel more comfortable, go to full tempo and see how the hips are moving **fluently and smoothly**.

Tip #33 – Flat feet

What is the position of the feet in Vertical Figure 8s?

During the vertical figure 8s try to have **both feet flat on the floor**.

When you first start practicing these movements, you will feel the need to lift each foot off the floor as the hip lifts, and the knee straightens.

If that is easier for you, you have permission to do it.

That way, the isolation will be **more visible**.

The other way is to make the vertical 8s with feet placed on the floor no matter the knees and hip movements.

Tip #34 – Bend the knees lower for improved isolation

To achieve it, before you start with the figure 8s, you have to **bend the knees lower** than in the standard belly dance posture. This will provide the hips with the necessary mobility and freedom to move.

As your muscles stretch up, you will gain more flexibility in the middle abs area, and your dancing will become more natural.

Tip #35 – Keep the upper part of the body static

Common for both horizontal and vertical figure 8s is having the upper part of the body still and static. There is no shoulder dropping, no additional chest lifting. All upperparts are relaxed, providing the hips with space to express the emotion.

Arms are not excluded from moving, but my advice is to do it once you have complete control of the hips and achieve the proper isolation.

How to Do Hip Locks and the Hip Drop

Hip Locks

In this session, we will cover the basic hip lock, which is also one very powerful step in belly dancing and allows different variations.

Now, since we have the necessary knowledge in hip lifting, we can move to the **hip lock.**

What is a hip lock?

A hip lock is **a sharp hip lift or a hop drop**. Lock movements, either in the upper or lower parts of the body, are powerful kicks with the hips or chests. With the lock, we want to emphasize the rhythm of the music, especially the drum.

Tip #36 - Listen to the music!

For a clearer illustration, imagine or even better, **turn on drum music** and try to catch the rhythm. Feel that whenever the drummer hits the drum, the sound is powerful and sharp.

This sound gives you the need to **imitate the same melody** using the body, in this case, the hips. Therefore, what we are trying to achieve is to make the music visible.

Every tone of the music has to be **interpreted with the body**. Just as singers share their message with words, dancers express their story through body movements.

That is why it is essential not just to hear the belly dancing music, but also to **understand and feel it**. Let your hips express the volume and the intensity of the drums.

Going back to the hip lock, every time you lift the hip, make it very sharp on each side. You will look very strong and confident in your steps, which I am sure that everyone is trying to achieve.

As mentioned before, there are many variations with the hip locks. Here we will explore the double hip lock.

Double Hip Locks

Tip #37 - Make Double hip lock using the hip lift technique

Let's imagine the basic belly dance posture again.

- As the knees are bent, start lifting the **left hip** and release it to center, then lift it again and release it. With each hip lift, the left knee straightens softly.
- As you notice, there are two accents on one side with the same hip.

- Then try with the **right hip**. Straighten the right leg and, at the same time, lift the right hip and release it to center, then lift it again and release it back to the center.
- Make sure that lifting is very **sharp** on each hip.
- During all these movements, keep the **feet steady** on the ground.
- **The body's weight** is between the two feet, and it does not shift from one foot to another.

- So, try the lifts again: left – left; right – right.

In the beginning, you may want to shift the weight on the left or right leg to get better isolation on each hip, and that is completely fine.

With time and practice, you will start feeling the bodyweight during this performance. Also, you will learn to do these hip locks with the weight split between the two feet.

Once again, this is **only** a hip movement, so make sure to avoid any motion with the upper part of the body and head.

Arms are opened out and relaxed, allowing the energy to come throughout the fingertips.

Hip Drop

Now, let's pay attention to one fundamental movement: **hip drops**. Once you have understood this step, you can feel that it has given you a solid ground to make variations.

Tip #38 – Drop the hip!

Belly dance posture. So, let's stand in the basic belly dance posture, feet are underneath the hips, knees bent, tailbone under, low abs tucked, chests lifted, head up, arms are open all the way out and relaxed.

- Shift the whole **weight** of your body on the right foot,

- Make small **step forward** with the left leg in front of you and

- **Touch the floor** with the left finger toe keeping the left heel lifted during this step.
- Try to **open the left foot** to the left side as much as you can. I know that it might feel like an unnatural position at the beginning, but within time and practice, you will improve it and start doing it correctly, even unconsciously. So, please be patient.

- **Bend both knees**, even more than in the basic belly dance posture.

- Especially bend down the right knee (supporting leg) and keep it bent all the way throughout this movement.

- While you are standing in this position, you will feel like burning in your **right glute**. This is very important because otherwise, you will not be able to isolate the hip with a straight leg. The more the knee is bent, the better the isolation becomes.

- Start **shifting** your weight from the right foot to the left leg (toe). You will feel the pressure from the weight on the left foot toe (ball) because the heel is all the way up.

- This shifting of the bodyweight will straighten the right leg allowing the left hip to be lifted. (That is very normal and natural),

- Nevertheless, even though, give yourself the effort to keep the **right knee bent**. You can do it!

- Lift the **left hip**, imagining that the hip wants to meet the rib cage bone. You will feel the engagement in the oblique muscles.

- Now, start releasing the hip down and **drop it**. Again, lift the hip and drop it down.

- Don't forget to keep the supporting leg bent, no matter of all the movements.

- Try the hip drop with the right leg forward, following all previous steps.

In the beginning, while you are practicing this movement, try it doing **slowly**. Be aware all the time of the weight shifts, about your position, and most importantly - do not forget to breathe.

Tip #39 – Sharpen the hip drop

Once you feel more confident (which I am sure you will very soon), make those hip drops **sharper**. Give accent to the drop. Drop and drop and drop. Make it visible. As you feel more confident, switch to tempo and do the drops even faster. Remember, the hips do this movement; the upper part of the body is relaxed and not moving.

Hip drop is one of my favorite movements in belly dancing. It opens your sensuality and gives space for your feminine energy to expand. The dancer can use many variations in choreography; in this case, we will cover the variation with a kick and with bent knee lifted.

Hip Drop & Kick

Starting position: We are starting from the previous position with the hip drops. So, keep your knees bent shifting the weight to the right foot (which is stationary and supporting leg), the left foot is in front, the toe is touching the floor, the left heel is up, tailbone under, lower abs tucked in, chest lifted, head up, and arms wide open out and soft.

- Lift the left hip up and drop it down
- Again, the left hip simultaneously goes up, preparing for the new drop.
- While hip is dropping down, release the left foot out for a kick.
- The released leg should become straight but elegant.

Tip # 40 - 'The Football Player'

Avoid throwing your leg in an uncontrolled way; instead, try to be present in the moment and focus on the foot.

Imagine that you are playing football (soccer) and you want to shot. You have to do almost the same movement.

One rule has to be applied to achieve the elegance in this step: when you release the leg, open the foot to the left and point the toe to the left.

- Come back to the starting position with the left toe touching the floor and drop the left hip down. Then again, hip goes up, kick the foot out, and drop the hip down.

- Notice that when you release the left leg for a kick, the **hip also drops down** at the same time with the kick. This is because the hip drops continuously like a regular, standard hip drop that we learned before, and therefore it has to continue no matter what the foot is doing.

- The foot can either be **static** (toe touching the floor) or **moving** (in the form of a kick) but the hip is dropping all the time, regardless of the foot position.

- Try all of these steps with the right leg and check which one fits you the most.

That is why it is essential to have a strong supporting leg that is bent during this movement. The burn in the glutes will increase because of the pressure on the right leg, but you will endure it. The pain will become so irrelevant once you see the result from your effort.

Hip drop & kick is a cycle that is repeating and has to be performed very smoothly without any significant pausing among the transitions.

Just to remind you that this is **only a hip movement**, and you should avoid all bouncing with the body. So, keep your upper part of the body static and relaxed.

Hip drop & Kick

1. Stand on the toes and drop the hip down

2. Drop the hip and kick the foot

Hip Drop with Bent Knee Lifted

Tip #41 – Lift the knee up instead of kicking it out

Let's come to the starting position for hip drop.

- Lift the left hip up, and then drop it down.

- Hip comes up again, and what follows is kicking the foot out.

- Instead of a kick, this time, keep the knee bent and lift it up, pointing the toes down.

- Lift the knee up for about 6-7 inches (15cm-20cm) from the floor.

- As you lift your knee, your hip drops down (in the previous case, you release the leg for a kick, and the hips drop down).

- Again, hips are continuing to drop and lift no matter of the foot position. I want to underline again the importance of keeping your support leg (stationary leg) bent all the time even if it straightens a bit when the hip goes up.

Hip drops with its variations are very feminine movements and take time to improve. Their performing should look effortlessly, gently, naturally.

My advice is to always practice with music. In the beginning, try slow-paced music, listen to the rhythm, and make the movements accordingly. Within time, you can challenge yourself with faster music, and for sure, you will notice the improvements.

Hip drop with bent knee lifted

1. Stand on the toes and drop the hip down

2. Drop the hip and lift the bent knee

Belly Dance Shimmy

Why is shimmy so unique?

Shimmy is, for me, the most challenging movement in belly dancing. The nice vibration that comes from the knees will transform you into an even more mesmerizing dancer, and the audience will fall in love with this part of the choreography.

How long does it take to be improved?

Shimmy takes quite a long period to be improved. You will need weeks, months, or years of practice. By telling you this, my point is not to discourage you, but rather to consider it as a challenge for you to become better with more practice.

What differs a good shimmy dancer from a bad shimmy dancer?

It is practice. You can achieve this movement through persistence and patience. Once you master the shimmy, you can use it to create different types of variations with the upper part of the body, or even with the hips and legs.

In this section, we will cover one basic and powerful shimmy: the Egyptian shimmy.

Egyptian Shimmy

Belly dance posture. So, let's stand in the basic belly dance posture, feet are underneath the hips, knees are softly bent, tailbone under, low abs tucked, chest lifted, head up, arms are open all the way out and relaxed.

Tip #42 – Generate motion with your knees, not with the hips!

In this movement, our focus will be ONLY on the knees and the motion that they produce.

It means that the hips are going to be excluded, and whatever happens in this area will only be a reflection of the movement of your knees.

As you are standing in the basic posture, it is of great importance to keep the knees very, but very soft, as you usually do for a walk.

- Bend your **left knee forward** and notice how the opposite leg is about to become straightened and locked.

- Do not lock the right leg, but again keep it very soft when you are straightening it backward.

Egyptian shimmy 1/2

1. Bend the left knee
forwards

- Then bend the right knee and straighten the left one. Continue to make this move as slow as possible, ...bending one leg at a time.

2. Bend the right knee
forwards

- Pay attention to the hips; they are not moving, aren't they? Keep them relaxed and still, don't lift, twist, or slide.

- Keep moving the knees and slowly increase the speed.

- Also, keep in mind that the upper part of the body is not moving along with the knees or bouncing in space.

What to expect in the early stages of learning shimmy?

You are not going to master the shimmy overnight. You may find your body in an unpleasant posture; there may be some tension in the glutes, struggles to coordinate the knees, etc. These are all real issues that every dancer faces at the beginning, during, and after their dancing career.

Tip #43 – Exercise on the floor

Here is one tip that worked for me, and I believe you can use it as well.

- **Sit** on the floor, lay, and straighten the legs.

- Lean the upper part of the body a little bit backward.

- Start **lifting** the left knee from the floor and then release it and put it down on the floor.

- To avoid any **knee injuries**, when putting the knee back on the floor, do not make it firm completely, but try to make some space between the floor and the knee.

- Lift the **right knee** up and release. After you make several up and down, tease yourself and go on a greater intensity.

- Your goal is to reach a **flow** between the knees and legs, a simultaneous movement that looks relaxed and effortless.

- Do this exercise for about 5-10 minutes **each day.**

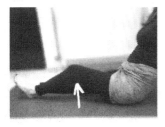

1. Lift the left knee of the floor

2. Lift the right knee of the floor

There is a lot of parts in this movement, but the goal is to do it without any tension, pressure, or even injury.

After you engage every atom of your body to improve yourself, you realize the complexity of this movement and the attention that is necessary to perform this in the best possible way.

Tip #44 - Avoid the following mistakes while performing the shimmy:

First, do not be afraid to bend the knee forward, make a strong strike with the knee, and get it out of its comfort zone. Do the same with both knees. You may feel the need to lock the knees and still make some movements, but that will appear as a vibration instead of shimmy. Vibration is more of a variation of the shimmy.

Second, maintain the balance of the feet. As you make the shimmy, you might find the upper part of the body leaning backward, which may cause pain in the lower back area. Another mistake to avoid is shifting the weight on the ball of the feet. That will result in excessive leaning of the upper part of the body to the front. Whenever you lose yourself in some of these positions, stop for a second, reconsider the process and start over again.

Third, try to relax the muscles and the entire body as much as you can. I know that it may look like a mission impossible from this perspective, but squeezing the glutes or keeping the knees almost locked, will cause you pain and frustration.

The process of enhancing shimmy MUST be fun, do not forget it.

Shimmy whenever you can and wherever you can. Make it your routine. Shimmy, while you are waiting for a bus or standing in front of the mirror. When you feel that the energy is coming from you, please do not stop it. Just release it and enjoy it!

Review

1. Basic belly dance hip movements: **hip twist** and **hip slides** (parallel to the floor) and **hip lifts** (lifting the hip up, as it wants to meet the rib cage). In all of the three movements, try to keep the feet stable on the

floor.

2. **Hip circles**: large circles (parallel to the floor). Create the circles out of your natural body alignment, meeting and connecting all four points of the cross in which center you are standing in (use the imagination and visualization). Small circles are created within your natural body alignment and involve hip lifts instead of hip slides and twist.

3. We **open the hip** on the left and close it on the right side. Why? Because of the duality in the human body equilibrium and the division between the female and male energy. Within time, you will start noticing that most of the movements, when performed with the left hip or leg, look more natural compared to the right side. However, practice enough on both sides to reach the balance.

4. Imagine the **infinity sign** ∞ when you are doing figure 8s. Horizontal 8s are parallel on the surface beneath you and include hip twist and hip slide. Vertical 8s require hip lifts and hip slides.

5. **Hip locks** are sharp, hip lifts, or hip drops. They are strong hip hits on each side. Variation of the hip drop is either with a kick or with a knee lift.

6. **Shimmy:** shake the knees, and only the knees. Your belly will shake too but as a reaction of the knees motion. Breathe and relax the body;

don't freeze yourself.

7. Choose your favorite **belly dance music**, and enjoy your practice.

8. Be gentle and **respectful** towards your body!

Chapter 3: Belly Dancing Tips for the Upper Part of the Body

How to Do the Belly Dance Head Shake

Belly dancing does not include only hip and leg movements; it requires coordination of almost every part of the body.

By activating the entire body, the dance itself will look as a whole. It is of great importance to developing skills that involve the upper part of the body, so let's start with incorporating the head movement, known as a head shake.

Belly Dance Head Shake

Tip #45 - Avoid Indian headshake!

One of the most used head movements is the Indian head shake, which we use on almost every party when we are in an element and show off our dancing skills. It includes sliding the head from one side to another. Since that type of belly dancing has not been subject to our belly dancing guide, in this section, we will cover the basic belly dance headshake.

Belly dance posture. Start with the basic belly dance posture; feet are in the width of the hips, knees are softly bent, tailbone down, lower abdominal tucked in, chest lifted, chin up, arms are opened and relaxed.

Having the arms spread and the shoulders relaxed:

- **Lean your head** on the left, as if you want to meet the left ear with the left shoulder. Leaning should be gentle; remember you are not aiming to reach the ear, just softly leaning. Then try it on the right side following the same steps.

- The transition from one to another side must be very **soft and smooth**, almost effortlessly.

Tip #46 - 'The Disapproval' Trick

Here is one tip that I am sure you will find helpful. Do you remember when your parents were about to give you punishment or disapproval and didn't want to accept it? They would have used a shaking point-finger to express their madness.

Also, you can do a headshake after the finger shake. Do the head shake more gently.

Imagine that you are in your parents' role and want to say to your child: "I know you are not telling the truth, but I'll find out". Most importantly, imagine the emotion while expressing these words. You do not have to be extremely mad, but a little bit provoked.

How to Do Chest Slides

We are going to explore the slide movements and see how they apply to the chest. Do you remember hip slides? Well, it happens the same with the chest, moving them from side to side.

Chest-Slide-Side-To-Side

Belly dance posture. So, let's get back to the belly dance posture and keep the hips out of every motion. Now is time for the hips to rest, and we want them to be still and stable.

Tip #47 – 'The String' Trick

- Slide the entire rib cage on the left, imagining a **string** going through the rib cage inside and the chest.

- Furthermore, imagine that someone is **pulling** out that string to the left. Allow your chest to follow the string and bring it on the left side.

- Sliding will engage **squeezing** the oblique muscles and the upper back muscles. Bring the chest back to neutral and now shift on the right side.

- Let the string be pulled out on the right and move the chest along with it.

One thing is essential: when sliding from side to side, keep the rib cage parallel with the floor and avoid any curvature of the body that will get you out of the desired position.

Tip #48 – Practice slowly!

Have one rule in mind: whenever you start practicing new movement, do it very **slowly**.

Make sure that your body is in the correct posture and that you understand the movements.

Visualize those movements in your mind, copy from there and paste them in the real moment. After you make several attempts of trying and reaching the goal, add some speed, and increase the pace. In this case, when you feel more comfortable challenging yourself doing the slides faster.

Chest slide-to-the-side

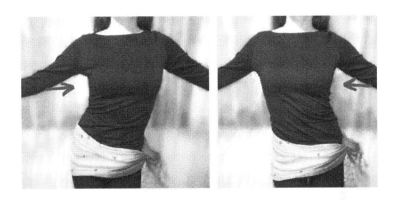

Chest-Slide-To-The-Front

Similar to the hips going forward, chest slide-to-the-front will practically do the same.

- While standing in the basic belly dance posture, imagine the string is going through the chest, entering the area between the **breasts** and exiting somewhere between the **shoulder blades**.

- Then, someone starts pulling the string out, causing your upper part of the body to get out of the natural alignment and to move **forward**.

- This movement will engage the inner middle back muscles that support the spine, and you will find the spine feel strong and firm.

Chest-slide-to-the-front

1. Move forwards the upper part of the body

- Then bring the chest back to neutral and try over again.

During this process, do not forget to keep the hips still no matter what the upper part of the body is doing. Moreover, yes, do not forget the most important key is to keep breathing.

How to Do Chest Lifts and Drops

Chest-lifts and drops correspond to the hip lifts and drops. If chest slides were movements to the left and the right, chest lifts/drops are movements up and down.

Stand in the basic belly dance posture, and imagine that you have a string going through your **breastbone**.

Tip #49 - 'The Necklace' Trick

- Imagine that you have a **necklace** – medium length, hanged over your neck.

- The rock from the necklace is falling in the **middle** of the ribcage, where the breasts are starting.

- Let's pretend that on the spot where the rock is, there is our **string**.

- Then, someone starts to **pull** the string **up** and to pull the ribcage along with it.

- Using the upper **abs** and the **diaphragm**, start lifting the ribcage upwards.

Chest lift and drops

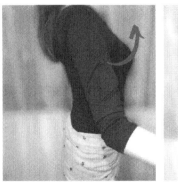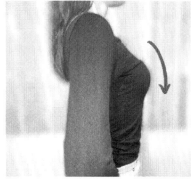

Tip #50 – Control the breathing

In the beginning, you may find yourself the need to synchronize the lifting with the inhaling.

It comes very naturally that whenever you want to lift the chest up, you have to inhale to provide that lifting.

In belly dancing, that is wrong because if you have to perform several lifts/drops and if you take a breath on each lift, you **risk yourself to lose the breath**, to feel dizzy, and the audience will get the impression that you are struggling for breath instead of enjoying the dance.

That is why it is essential to practice this lifting without constantly inhaling.

Tip #51 – Feel the burning in the back muscles

Keep the arms relaxed and open in a low V position, shoulders pointing backward and down, lift the chest up, and feel which group of back muscles are being engaged.

Those muscles surround the area of the middle part of the spine.

You will feel a light burning in the muscles between the shoulder blades. Regarding the shoulder blades, they are not engaged at all.

Remember that you do not have to squeeze the shoulders backward, but to use the upper abdominal muscles and the diaphragm to lift and open the chest.

Chest dropping will be yourself releasing to the neutral position.

Lift the chest up and release. Repeat it several times. Do not forget to keep the shoulders down, and still, hips are not moving at all, and you are not bouncing in space.

This technique takes time to practice, always be present in the moment, and control your breathing. In the beginning, it may seem to you that it is too hard to achieve, but believe me, continuous practice will be the key to success.

Chest Lock

One beautiful movement that comes out of chest lifts and drops is the chest lock.

Tip #52 - When to use a chest lock?

You want to use a check lock when you want to emphasize the sound, especially the drum. The beauty of this movement comes from the performer's ability to isolate the chest and move it independently. It is as if the dancer is playing with this part of the body, popping and dropping along with the music's rhythm.

When we were working on the hips in the previous chapter, hip locks were sharp hip lifts and hip drops. Parallel on that, **chest locks are sharp chest lifts and drops**.

Belly dance posture. Start with the basic belly dance posture; feet are in the width of the hips, knees are softly bent, tailbone down, lower abdominal tucked in, chest lifted, chin up, arms are opened and relaxed.

- Take a standard breath (as you usually do) and try to hold it for a few seconds.

- Those seconds of holding the breath are where the chest lift happens.

- Lift the chest up, as described before, but this time try to exaggerate the lifting, making it very **sharp**. The feeling is like as you are **hiccupping** (without the hiccup sound, of course).

- When we hiccup, the chest lifts up very sharply, but involuntary and uncontrolled.

- Instead of that, be present while you are lifting the chest, focus, and raise it sharply.

- As the chest is up, exhale, but be careful not to drop it down while you keep chest still up. Once you have exhaled, drop the chest sharply down to its neutral position.

- The dropping down has to be a result of releasing the upper abs.

Keep trying this technique even when you are not dancing. Practice whenever you can, wherever you can, and as long as you can. If you feel that you are getting tired very quickly, do not panic, it is normal and is part of this process.

How to Do Chest Circles

Do you remember the hip circles? In that section, we were describing the hip positions in the large hip circle and then in the small hip circle.

Very similar to hip circles are chest circles. They are a combination of **chest slides** and **chest lifts**.

Depending on the combination of these two separate movements, there are **horizontal chest circles** and **vertical chest circles**.

Horizontal Chest Circle

Horizontal chest circles are also known as large chest circles because they engage moving the entire ribcage and are performed outside of the natural body alignment.

Belly dance posture. Let's stand in the basic belly dance posture; feet are underneath the hips, knees are softly bent, tailbone under, low abs tucked, chest lifted, head up, arms are open all the way out and relaxed. Lift the shoulders up, roll them backward and release down.

Tip #53 – Combine chest slides to the side with chest slide to the front

Now is time to use the chest-slide techniques that we have described before. Horizontal chest circles are a combination of chest-slide-side-to-side and chest-slide-to-the-front.

It means that we have to connect **four different points** to create the circle.

First point is on the left side; the second point is reaching the forward side, then is the right side, and the last point is bringing the chest back to the neutral position.

During chest circles, these four points have to be **smoothly connected** into a nice circle. If you feel some insecurities about these two movements, please refer to the section and explanations above.

Tip #54 – Start the horizontal chest circle

Using the imaginary **string** that is passing throughout the ribcage (breasts height), feel that someone is pulling it to the left.

This pulling engages the right group of oblique muscles, and you almost feel the squeezing on the right part of the body.

From this (first) position, move the chest forward using the middle back muscles surrounding the spine and the diaphragm.

What do you have to avoid by now?

Do not use your shoulders to bring the chest forward, instead use the middle back muscles to push the ribcage in front.

If everything is done correctly, at this moment, your chest is standing out of your natural body alignment.

The next point you have to reach is the **right side**, so start moving your chest all the way to the right.

Your chest has to be in the right chest slide position to ensure that you are standing correctly.

That will engage the left group of oblique muscles, and you will feel the squeezing on the left side of the body.

To complete the chest circulation, just release it to the center (neutral position).

Horizontal chest circle

1. Slide your chest to the left

2. Move your chest to the front

3. Slide your chest to the right, and release to neutral

Tip #55 – Do not concave the spine!

Avoid this mistake:

Another mistake you have to avoid here is concaving the upper part of the body when bringing the chest in the center, so you don't end up in the position of the letter 'C.'

It is not necessary to curve the upper part of the spine or to engage the shoulders whenever you have to release the chest back in the center.

- Start the circle over again, reach all four points very smoothly and challenge yourself to do the chest circles continuously.

- Whenever you feel more confident, do it faster and reverse on the other side.

- Notice that as the pace increases, chest circles are getting smaller and smaller.

Tip #56 – Keep these chest movements parallel with the floor

Horizontal chest circles, as the name itself indicates, are parallel to the floor. They are not lifts and drops because that is a different type of chest circle.

Remember to keep your hips steady and still while chest circulates and eventually practice your breathing process. Try not to use the breath whenever you work with the chest. Breathe normally, and don't spare the diaphragm; let it work for you.

Vertical Chest Circles

The second type of chest circles is the vertical circle. It is a combination of two movements that were explained earlier: chest-slide-side-to-side and chest-lifts-and-drops.

In this section, to create the circles, we have **to connect four points** differently.

Tip #57 - 'The Rhombus Sign'

First, we bring the chest to the left side, then lift up, slide to the right side, and, at last, release it in the neutral position.

When all four points are connected, they should look like a rhombus sign: à. By smoothing the connection of these points, we create a vertical chest circle.

Vertical chest circle

Imagine the Rhombus sign in front of you

Before you begin, please repeat the movements that we are about to use in the next steps. If you find any difficulties with these movements, please go back to the sections where you can find the explanations and continue with this type of chest circle.

Stand in the basic belly dance posture, which I am sure that by now, you know it by heart.

- Pay attention to the **shoulders**. Lift them up, roll back and drop down. Arms are opened out and resting relaxed in a smooth 'V' position.

- Start by sliding the chest on the **left side** engaging the right oblique muscles next to your ribcage (first position)

- **Lift** the chest up to reach the second point.

- Continue to the third point, which is sliding the chest to the **right side**.

- In the end, **release** the chest and bring it to the neutral position.

Vertical chest circle

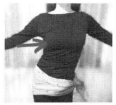

1. Slide your chest to the left

2. Lift your chest up

3. Slide your chest to the right

4. Release your chest down to neutral

Do you remember what we have emphasized while lifting the chest up? - The middle back muscles surrounding the spine.

These muscles are providers of chest lifting and chest opening. Do not forget to use the diaphragm to help you with the lifts.

You should avoid using the breath to lift the chest and use the shoulders to open the chest.

Regarding the dropping of the chest down (the fourth point), make sure not to curve the upper part of the back backward. It has to be a smooth releasing of the chest to the center (neutral position).

Try to connect these chest circles one after another, then make the right side to be your first starting position and start the cycle again.

Vertical chest circles also require still and steady hips, relaxed neck, and controlled shoulders.

Let's Figure 8 with the Upper part of the Body

If you have thought that the hip figure 8s were enough, you have lied.

I already have a new set of figure 8s for you, this time with the chest. They are super challenging and fun, and I hope that you will enjoy it. To perform this move, you should have acquired the basics of chest movements and some math.

As you are already guessing, there are two types of figure 8s: **horizontal and vertical chest figure 8s**.

Horizontal Chest Figure 8

Tip #58 - Combine chest slides and chest push forward

If this type of figure 8 is parallel to the floor, how to perform?

We are going to break this move into several parts so that you can pay attention to every detail that will be exposed.

Horizontal 8s combine chest slides and chest push forward, which I am sure that you have mastered these elements by now. If not, please refer to the sections above, and let's get started.

Belly dance posture. Stand in the basic belly dance posture; feet are underneath the hips, knees are softly bent, tailbone under, low abs tucked, chest lifted, head up, arms are open all the way out, and relaxed. Lift the shoulders up, roll them backward and release down.

Tip #59 - 'The Rectangle' Tip

Again, we are going to connect four different points to achieve this movement, so instead of the box that we have used for the hi████re 8s, imagine that you are standing in the center of a rectangle   (a lot of math, I know).

- Put that rectangle on your chest height and notice that you now have four points (two on the front and two on the backsides).

- Your goal is to reach with the chest for each of these points, connect them, and smooth into a nice infinity sign ∞.

- Start with a chest slide on the **left side**. Our first point to reach is the back left diagonal (A).

- **Twist** the chest to that point and keep it only horizontal. The left shoulder will go back along with the twist, and that is OK.

- From this position, we are moving to the second point, which is the **front left corner** of the rectangle (B).

- Slowly start twisting the chest forward and take the shoulder too. Be careful: we are still in a **sliding position**.

- It is important to **slide** the chest all the way to the front left corner, avoiding any central chest positioning.

- Your next point is the **right-back corner** (C), so slowly slide the chest towards this diagonal.

- Finish by twisting the chest to the **front right** (D), where the left shoulder will be pointing to the left-back corner waiting for the new, upcoming figure 8.

- Define these points in your mind and repeat the exercise for several times.

Once you have felt comfortable in the rectangle, smooth the connection of each point.

Bow the movements from point A to point B and from point C to point D.

Improving chest figure 8s takes time, so don't get discouraged or frustrated if you fail on your first attempts.

Tip #60 – Engage the oblique muscles

Work on **stretching the oblique muscles**, those are the wheels in these motions. You can go as far as you can stretch on each side.

Also, work parallel stretching on both sides. I feel that my left oblique muscles are more stretched, so I find the sliding and bowing on the right side much easier. When I slide to the left, and when I engage the right oblique, it is more difficult. However, I am sure that with more practice, this obstacle can be overcome too.

Vertical Chest Figure 8

Tip #61 – Combine the chest slide and the chest lift

Let's combine the chest slide and the chest lift. *What will happen?* A vertical chest figure 8. We are going to break this movement into a few parts that will help you to improve it faster.

How to make Vertical chest figure 8?

Stand in the basic belly dance posture, and make sure that the shoulders are lifted up, rolled back and dropped down. Keep the rectangle still in your mind, this time having it placed in front of you.

- We are going to slide the chest to the left side, and this is our point A. (Left down corner of the rectangle)

- From this position, we are preparing the chest for a lift upwards.

Instead of lifting the chest from the central position, lift the chest from the slide-to-the-left position.

- This means that the chest is slid on the left side and then lifted up from that position (B). To achieve it, use your middle back muscles. (Left up corner of the rectangle)

- Now, let's go through the central position of the body and slide on the right side. This is our third position C. (Right down corner of the rectangle)

- Next, lift the chest up from position C, and we are almost in the final position D. (Right up corner of the rectangle)

- You can also imagine these points as a **bow tie**. Reach each of the bow tie corners with the chest and repeat for few times.

- Bow the transition from point A to point B and from point C to point D.

- Smoothly connect the two parts of the bow tie (A&B and C&D) into one whole movement.

You probably noticed chest isolations are harder to achieve (at least, that was the case for me). Somehow, I feel that hip figure 8s are easier because the knees are of great help. Of course, it doesn't mean that we have to put away the chest and all the movements it brings along. One thing we do know for sure is to keep practicing and keep enjoying it.

Review

1. **Belly dance headshake** is the opposite of the Indian headshake. This shake includes a very smooth leaning of the head, from one side to another.

2. Imagine the string that goes throughout your chest to **slide** them from the left to the right. Use the oblique muscles whenever you stretch on each side. When it comes to the slide forward, engage the middle back muscles for a stronger push. Keep the shoulders still and avoid squeezing them backward.

3. **Chest lifts and drops** are only possible if you use the diaphragm and the middle back muscles to lift it up. Do not inhale and do not use the breath to lift the chest up. You will collapse after the third inhaling, trust me.

4. **Chest locks** are sharp chest slides and chest lifts/drops. They are very beautiful isolations that decorate your choreography.

5. **Chest circles** can be horizontal and vertical.

6. **Horizontal** or large chest circles are parallel with the floor and include chest slides to the side and chest push forward.

7. **Vertical** or small chest circles are a combination of chest slide and chest lift/drop.

8. **Chest figure 8s** can be horizontal and vertical.

9. **Horizontal figure 8s** are smooth connections of the sides of the rectangle. You will need the chest-slide-to-the-side, chest-slide-to-the-front, and a chest twist.

10. **Vertical figure 8s** are smooth connections of a bow tie corners. To do so, you use the chest slides and chest lifts.

Chapter 4: Belly Dancing Arms and Shoulders Techniques

We are moving into a new section in which we are still going to work on the upper part of the body.

Tip #62 - The beauty of the Arms

Some people may think that belly dancing is a dance that mainly involves the work of the hips and frankly said, the name itself indicates that belly dancing engages mostly the 'belly area'. Nevertheless, the reality is more different.

On one side, the accent is on hip movements, especially on shimmies and hip drops, but also on belly isolations and figure 8s. In general, all hip movements represent the capability, power, and creativity of the dancer.

However, none of this would have been completed without the upper part of the body's movements and the beauty it brings. All elements of the upper part of the body can be powerful as well. These movements are elegant and express the feminine energy in our bodies. You can express a lot of yourself to the audience with the use of your arms and with your hands.

In the next few sections, I am going to share with you some secrets of how to get the hands in a perfect belly dance position, so stay tuned.

How to Put Your Hands in the Correct Belly Dance Position

For the hands and palms exercises, you don't have to stay in the basic belly dance position. It is optional and depends on you. While dancing and performing, of course, the proper body position is very crucial.

Tip #63 – Put your hands in the basic belly dance hand position

Ok, so let's see the basic hands and fingers position in belly dancing.

- Gather your hands in a '**praying**' position, adding some space in between. Skip merging the hands.

- Keep the hands in their natural, neutral position.

- Fingers are not too tight, nor too loose.

- Start moving the **thumb** and bring it closer to the **middle finger**, but be careful and avoid any merging of these two fingers (middle finger and thumb).

- The thumb is getting closer to the middle finger. The middle finger **deviates** a little bit from the neutral position and softly drops down.

- The goal is to make these fingers **parallel** to each other.

- Meanwhile, the rest three fingers are standing in their normal position slightly **separated**. (Little fingers may spread out insignificantly, but it is completely normal).

What is the most common mistake?

You all know the famous Spanish instruments – Castanets. They are played by using the middle finger and the thumb, and these fingers are constantly touching each other. Well, this 'Castanets fingers position' is not common for belly dancing, and you should avoid it.

Instead of such drastic movements of the middle finger and the thumb, keep them gently separated with space in between.

Basic hand belly dance position

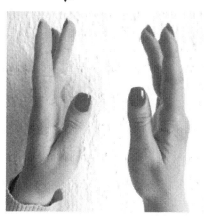

How to Make Fish and Snake Hand Position

There are two basic variations of the hands' position: fish and snake position.

These two positions have received their names because the movements of the hands imitate the movements of these two animals. They are super easy and can be combined in many variations in your choreography.

Fish Hand Position

Tip # 64 - 'Fish swim'

Firstly, in your mind, imagine doing a fish swim. Fish swim by flexing the body and the tailback and forth. Do this with your hands as well.

- Place the hand in a **handshake** position (like as you want to make a handshake with someone).

- Now, notice that the hand is consisted of two parts: **fingers** (the dynamic part) and **palm** – the static part.

- Based on the comparison to the fish anatomy, our fingers match with the fishtail, and palms match with the body of the fish.

- If the tail is the most active part of the fish, analogous to that fingers represent the most active part on our hand.

Now, let's start 'swimming' our hand fish.

- From this handshake position, start **concaving** all fingers together.

- Do not concave them completely, but keep the concavity for **45** degrees.

- Then, stretch the fingers **backward** also for 45 degrees.

Imagine that all of your five fingers point at 12 o'clock (while they are in their neutral position). Concaving forward means to bring them to 2 o'clock (softly folded). Stretching backward is placing the fingers from 2 o'clock to 10 o'clock (going backward 2-1-12-11-10

As you can notice, fingers move in a range of 10 – 2 o'clock. Also, see that as the fingers go to 10, the palm pushes softly forward (imitating the flexing of the fish).

It happens the same when fingers go in a **reverse** direction forward; the palm goes gently backward.

Fish hand position

1. Handshake position

2. Start concaving the fingers

3. Concave the fingers

4. Stretch the fingers backwards

When converting this movement into a **fluent transition** from one position to another, you see how elegant this move is. During these movements, it is crucial to keep the palm, hand, and arm relaxed.

Snake Hand Position

Tip #65 – Move your hands like a snake

This one is also a super-powerful position of the hands that will make you an outstanding performer.

- Put your hand in a position as if you want to show off your **nails** to someone. (Palm facing down)

- This is the first position A or a '**closed**' position.

- Then softly drop the hand downwards, imagining that you are giving your hand to someone for a **kiss**. This is the second position B.

- Then turn the hand on the opposite side, like as you **beg** for money. (Palm facing up)

- This is the third position C or '**opened**' position.

- All you have to do is to connect these three points A, B, and C.

- Please do not make this connection just a 'dead' rotation from A to B. Exaggerate it; bring some life, emotions, and softness in the hands.

Snake hand position

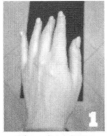

'Closed' position

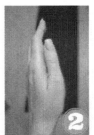

Palm facing up

You can practice these two hand positions without engaging the basic hand posture. Still, later you can add the beautiful finger position from the basic hand posture in belly dancing that was explained before.

Spread the Bird Arms (Snake Arms)

Arms are one of the most critical and essential parts of belly dancing. They are the key element when it comes to expressing emotions during performance.

A long time ago, in my very first beginnings, I was one of those people who have thought: *'well...ok, yes, maybe arms are an important part, but probably not as much as hips are'*.

Fortunately, very soon, I realized the importance of all the advantages of incorporating the arms in the dance.

Tip #66 - The Power of Arms

I believe just as singers use their voice to express their feelings and to deliver the story of the song, belly dancers use their arms to achieve the same result. Belly dancers speak with their arms, using them as a tool whenever they want to address the audience, whenever they want to start with something, or whenever they want to combine with other dance steps and variations.

The number one thing to remember when using the arms is to keep them as relaxed as possible.

I know that it sounds like a typical cliché, but trust me, this is all true and already tested.

The faster you become conscious about the state and position in which you keep your arms, the better you overcome this challenge, and you will be able to apply all the variations with the arms.

Sometimes, you may not be aware of how you move the arms, and you will not be sure if you keep them soft. My advice is to ask someone to watch you during your dance and let you know about that. If you do not feel that confident, you can record on your phone and observe your style later.

Tip #67 – Observe your movements

The **OBSERVATION** is crucial if you want to develop these skills for one simple reason: during the dance, we may think that we are the best performer ever, but seeing the dance from another person's perspective is good for your improvement. The point is not becoming dependent on others' opinions but instead becoming more self-critical and open for different views.

I was convinced that I was doing everything correctly until my teacher made me realize that actually, my arms were so tense that all my performance lost its beauty.

However, these mistakes are expected and normal at the beginning because you are trying to focus your attention on one part (hips, for example), and you cannot control the rest of the body spontaneously. Do not be discouraged from the challenges you may face in your early stages of learning; remember, it is part of the process, and you will be surprised at the speed you are going to overcome all of them, with practice, patience, and love.

In this section, we are going to find out the basic arms position in belly dancing. We will start with the so-called **'Bird arms.'** Then, we will explore its variation – the **'Snake arms.'**

Notice once again that we are going to **imitate** these two powerful animals' movements, and we can discover the possibilities of these movements for combination with other steps.

Before we start with the two styles of arm movements, first, let me guide you through the **four basic arm positions**.

Belly dance posture. Stand in the basic belly dance posture, keep the feet under the hips, softly bend the knees, tailbone tucked and facing down, lower abs engaged, chest lifted, shoulders rolled back and down, the chin lifted, head up and arms are opened in a soft low V position. Do not forget the hands and put the fingers in the necessary position (please check the section above regarding the basic hand position if you face any struggles).

Tip #68 - Arms position no. 1

Lift both of your hands **above** the head, imagining that you are holding a small ball in your arms.

Pay attention to the elbows; they have to be very soft and gently bent.

Hands are in a 'prayer' position, one inch (2,5 cm) separated from each other. This is the arm position number 1.

Tip #69 - Arms position no. 2

From this position, start dropping the left arm downwards until it reaches the position of letter 'L.'

The left-arm elbow is now angled under 90 degrees.

The left-hand remains in the starting position and faces towards the inside, looking towards your body.

Gently open (lean) the left arm in the elbow for about 10-15 degrees on the left.

Then shift the attention on the right arm and drop it down to the same position as the left one.

Tip #70 - Arms position no. 3

The third position is straightforward; turn the hands (palms) on the opposite side, facing outward. The movement here happens only in the wrist of the hand as it turns from the inside to the outside. It feels like making small circles only with the hands from downwards to upwards.

Tip #71 - Arms position no. 4

To achieve the fourth position, start dropping the arms from the third position in the following way:

- Keep the part of the upper arms parallel with the surface beneath.

- Then, twist and turn the forearms downwards. Drop the forearms down as if they are hanging. The upper arms are still parallel to the floor.

- Next, bring the palms close to your hips. Palms are now facing towards your body and bring them close to the hips (do not touch the hips with the palms, just place them close enough).

- As you move the palms towards the body, the elbows fall gently down.

- Notice that now, the upper arm and the forearm are in a strong 'V.' While you are standing in this position, elbows will naturally go backward.

- Instead, try to keep them facing **forward** as much as you can.

Four Arms Positions

During all of these positions, keep the hands in the basic belly dance hand posture. Otherwise, these movements are losing their elegance. Also, the beauty will be lost if the arms are not relaxed (I know I have said this a million times, I will say it one more time, forgive me).

Practice these positions consistently; make them a starting ritual whenever you decide to dance. Very soon, you will be aware of the combinations you can make with the rest of the steps discussed before.

Here is one **exercise**: combine the fourth arm position with the opening and closing hip movements. For the rest combinations, I trust in your capability and creativity. So do not wait, hit the floor, and do your best.

Bird arms style

We are going to pass on exploring the types of arm styles and techniques. The first one is the style of Bird arms.

Belly dance posture. Stand in the basic belly dance posture, keep the feet under the hips, softly bend the knees, tailbone tucked and facing down, lower abs engaged, chest lifted, shoulders rolled back and down, the chin lifted, head up, and arms opened and relaxed.

Tip #72 – Spread your arms like a bird

Start by releasing the arms down, as you usually do for a walk.

Slowly start lifting one arm and bring it above your head. Then slowly release it down and do the same with the opposite arm.

What is essential in this part?

Every time you lift the arm up, the hand (palm) is facing downwards, and when the arm is releasing down, the palm is facing on the side (all fingers point upwards).

Tip # 73 - 'Touching wall'

Imagine that you are touching a wall with the edges of your nails all the way up. Imagine that you are standing in an arm-length distance from the wall.

As you lift the arm up (fingers point down), feel the wall as if it is the most precious thing for you at that moment. Softly lift the arm up, be gentle with the wall, and at the same time, arc the arm in the elbow to make the lifting even more elegant.

Then, turn the hand so that all fingers (including the palm) are lying on the wall and even more gently, drop it all the way down. Try to develop this connection with the wall (or anything else, different subject or even a person), and try to transmit all the tenderness within you to them. These movements are full of softness and passion.

Remember, we are not lifting both arms all at once; instead, we lift and drop one arm after another. These transitions from one arm to another have to be smoothly and fluently, skipping all pausing in between. Bird arms should be opened, making a trajectory starting from the leg (your normal standing arm position) to the above of your head and reverse.

Bird arms position

Lifting arm + hand pointing down; Dropping arm + hand facing up

Snake Arms Style

Snake arms are variations of Bird arms. There are three points on the arm on which you have to focus all of your attention. Those are **shoulder**, **elbow,** and **wrist**.

Tip #74 – Move the arms like a snake

Stand in basic belly dance posture (including the arms) and

- Start lifting the left shoulder upwards, as if it wants to meet the ear. Do not bring it too close to the ear; keep it softly lifted (head is steady and stable all the time).

- Next, notice that by now, your left elbow is facing down. Well, we are going to switch this position from facing down to facing up.

- Rotate the elbow upwards, engaging the triceps muscles of the arm.

- Next, you have to notice that, in this position, the left wrist is pointing down, and guess what, we want to change its position and face it upwards too.

- As the wrist points up, the elbow naturally falls (otherwise, you will not be able to lift the wrist). So, lift the left wrist up, and what do you notice about the hand? It is almost in the position of a Bird arm style (fingers pointing down).

- The hand in snake arms is pointing down too, and as the wrist lifts up, the palm rolls and opens just like as it is going to be laid on the wall (fingers point up - check in Bird-arms section).

- Repeat this snake arm a few times more before you switch and do the same with the right arm.

By now, we have created one part of the snake arms – the lifting. To make the snake complete, we need the reverse process of releasing the arm down.

Luckily, the releasement comes very naturally, and there isn't any big issue. All three points (shoulder, elbow, and wrist) are reversing to their starting positions.

- Let's continue from the first part of the snake arms.
- After we have lifted the arm correctly, slowly release the shoulder, the elbow, and the wrist to their neutral positions.
- During the releasing down, the palm is opened all the way to outwardly and touches the imaginary wall with all five fingers.

In snake arms style, same as in bird style, the arms are going one after another. As the left one lifts, the right one releases and reverses.

Tip #75 – Flowing snake arms

The most important key in this style is the **FLOW**. Only when you maintain the flow with the arms, the snake appears.

Snake arms position

1.Shoulder lifts up

2. Elbow lifts up

3. Wrist lifts up

Tip #76 – Arms styles in practice

How and when to use arm styles?

You can take advantage of these arm styles in various combinations. Bird arms can be soft and gentle on the one hand, and on the other hand, they can be very vivid and wide, especially when you want to exaggerate some part in the choreography.

You can use bird arms whenever you want to look big during the performance (depending on the music and the flow), and one way to achieve that look is to stand on the ball of the feet and then spread the arms and use it as your wings.

Snake arms are very gentle and elegant. I find this style very useful in slow pace music because the slower they are performed, the more powerful they become, at least for me. Although snake arms may appear as easy arm movements, do not underestimate it, especially when you combine with other steps. Once we are out of focus and concentration, we can easily get out of any position.

Shoulders Position in Belly Dance

Another beautiful isolation that comes from the upper part of the body is the shoulder isolation. As you can notice, we are trying to isolate and to become aware of as more elements/ parts on our body. Someone may think that shoulders do not offer any specific movement, but let me tell you that with shoulders, you can do almost everything you tried with the hips or chest. So, let's start from the beginning.

Belly dance posture. Stand in the basic belly dance posture and keep the shoulders very relaxed. Lift them up, roll back and release down.

Four Shoulder Isolations

Next, we are going to discover four different positions of the shoulders (four different isolations).

- From the starting position, **lift** one shoulder up. Make the lifting, like as you want to reach the ear. Avoid any leaning of the head downwards; keep it steady and centered. Lift the shoulder and release it to become neutral. **(Position no. 1)**

- Then, push the shoulder forward as much as your muscles allow and release it to regular. **(Position no. 2)**

During all these four isolations, we are using only the shoulder muscles (including the shoulder blade behind).

- In the third position, the shoulder is pushing backward, engaging the lower shoulder muscle and bring it back to neutral. **(Position no. 3)**

- Forth position is dropping the shoulder downwards from the regular position. Although a very small movement, it is visible. **(Position no. 4)**

Four Shoulder Isolations

1. Lift the shoulder up

2. Push the shoulder to the front
2. Push the shoulder to the front

3. Push the shoulder to the back

4. Slightly push the shoulder down

During these isolations, elbows and wrist are down and each of the four isolations do not reflect on their position. Practice these four pushes with both shoulders (one after another), have fun, and start thinking about the possibilities in which you can apply these movements.

How to Do Shoulder Shimmy

Are you people ready for a new type of shimmy?

This one is as thrilling as the hip shimmy. I found it very easy to understand, and it consists of elements that we discussed before.

Belly dance posture. So stand in the basic belly dance posture, have your shoulders relaxed, and rolled back down. Arms are in a soft low V position. Elbows and wrists are facing down. Palms are relaxed in their position.

Tip #77 – Connect the shoulders into a flowing movement

Imagine that your shoulders are connected with a string. This means that they are not isolated one from another; instead, they are working as a team.

If there is an action of the left shoulder, the right one reacts.

Having this in mind, push the left shoulder forward. As this shoulder goes forward, the right one retreats and pushes backward.

Come to the neutral position and now do the same movement with the right shoulder. Push it forward and, at the same time, pull the left one backward.

Tip #78 – Make sure you are not missing anything

Remember three things:

1. First, keep the elbows and the wrists in their basic belly dance posture. Avoid any need to move the forearm forward or backward along with the shoulder.

2. Second, the motion happens only by the shoulders. All other parts of the body are still and stable.

3. Thirdly, avoid any exaggerated twisting of the spine. Engage the muscles on the shoulder blades to produce these pushes.

Practice these shoulders, pushing very slowly. Whenever you feel confident, increase speed. Once you have hit tempo, you are doing the shimmy shoulders. Congratulations!

Review

1. **Basic belly dance hand position**: move the thumb and bring it closer to the middle finger without merging these two fingers. The goal is to make these fingers parallel to each other. Meanwhile, the rest three fingers are standing in their normal position slightly separated.

2. **Fish hand position**: first, put the hand in a handshake position. Second, move the four fingers to 2 o'clock and then backward to 10 o'clock. Third, fingers concave softly when going to 2 o'clock and extend when reaching 10 on the backward.

3. **Snake hand position**: the inner of the palm points downwards, then hand gently drops (waiting for a kiss), and then palm turns

upwards. These are the three positions that we want to meet. Softly turn the palm from the inside to the outside and then reverse. The key of this hand position is in the transition from A to C. Make it gentle and soft.

4. **There are four arm positions**: first, arms lifted above the head; second, upper arms are dropped and parallel with the floor, forearms softly points up and outwards; third, palms turn from the inside to the outside, make a small circle with the hands; fourth, forearms drop down, and palms are close to the hips.

5. **Bird arms style**: Your arms are gently touching a wall with the edges of the nails. When the arm lifts, the hand points down with all fingers. When the arm drops down, the entire extended hand, along with the fingers point upwards.

6. **Snake arms style**: important are three points – shoulder, elbow, and wrist. First, lift the shoulder, then elbow points up, and at last, wrist comes up too. The real snake arm appears when you create a synchronicity between the raising and dropping arm.

7. There are four basic **shoulder isolations**: lifting upward, pushing forward, pulling backward, and dropping downward.

8. **Shoulder shimmy**: imagine a string connecting both of the shoulders. As one shoulder pushes forward, the other one goes backward in the opposite diagonal. If this

motion is speeded up, the result is a perfect shoulder shimmy.

9. Whenever you work on the shoulder area, keep the **head** and the **neck muscles** calm and soft.

10. Working on the shoulder area requires having **still** hips and **a controlled** body.

Chapter 5: Belly dance isolations

The word 'isolation,' many times, has been used whenever we want to focus and work only on one part of the body.

Tip #79 – Understanding the isolation

The word isolation, by itself, means to separate one part (it can be an individual or a subject) from the whole.

In belly dancing, the term isolation is used to describe the state of separating one part (element) of the body from the rest.

Example: If our goal is to isolate the hips, our attention and focus should be just towards the hips. Hips will be the only part that is moving in that particular moment. The same formula applies when isolating the body's other elements (chest, shoulders, head, arms, and hands).

All the beauty of belly dancing comes from these isolations, at least for me. That is a challenge on which you have to be proud every time you achieve it and lifts you one level up. However, keep in mind that it is an ongoing process requiring improvements on a daily level.

My story with belly dance isolations...

Every time I see a belly dancer performing some choreography, I get so astonished by the ease, smoothens, and the elegance of their isolations. It looks out of all human standards and capabilities, and I end up thinking: wow, how is that possible?

In the early stages of my belly dancing journey, I thought moves and isolations could only be performed by a gifted dancer such as someone who has a natural talent in belly dancing. I felt that some techniques could never be achieved and were reserved only for the chosen ones.

Luckily, it did not take long to realize that this consideration is unproductive and destructive. It keeps you locked safe in the comfort zone, discouraging you from any progress. However, I had no intention to remain in this position for a long time. I was determined to give the maximum effort, using every single atom of the body to go even further from yesterday.

As no change happens overnight, so it is with the isolations. You cannot expect quick results and do not get frustrated if it takes a longer period. It is different for everyone and depends on the time consumed on practicing, the flexibility, and, most importantly, of the willingness to learn and your passion for the dance.

Cherish each new improvement and every obstacle overcome. It is a victory over your limitations, which has to be rewarded with appreciation and gratitude.

I hope that I have given you enough encouragement to continue with the next challenge: *belly isolation*.

Our focus will be only on the belly and on achieving isolation of three groups of muscles: upper, middle, and lower abdominal muscles. You may ask: is it possible? Yes, it is, and in the next section, I will show you how.

What is Belly Isolation?

Before we continue with the isolation of different belly muscles, focus first on isolating the entire abdominal.

Belly dance posture. Stand in the basic belly dance posture, keep the feet under the hips, softly bend the knees, tailbone tucked and facing down, lower abs engaged, chest lifted, shoulders rolled back and down, the chin lifted, head up, and arms opened and relaxed in a low V position.

Belly isolation means that we are going to move only the belly while the rest of the body is relaxing. How to achieve it? In a very simple way by contracting and releasing the abdominal muscles. This isolation is only a muscle isolation, and no other part of the body will be engaged to support or ease this motion.

Tip #80 - 'The Punch'

Imagine that someone is punching you in the stomach. The natural body reaction of the punching is contracting the abdominal muscles to protect the organs inside.

Luckily, in this exercise, no one will punch you, but you have to imitate the muscle contraction and to pull of the belly inside.

Tip #81 - 'The Bikini Photoshoot' Trick

If you want, you can use this tip too: have you ever found yourself in a situation when suddenly someone wants to take a photo of you while you are in a bikini? I believe we all have. In that sudden moment, we instantly pull the belly inside to show off the six packs (or some leftovers). Well, that kind of contraction I want you to produce when you isolate the belly in belly dancing.

- So, pull the belly in, engage all abdominal muscles, and release.

- Remember to keep the rest part of the body super still, especially hips. Avoid any need to move the pelvis area along with the belly contraction.

- For better support, place your hands on the hips. This way, you will be more in control of what is going on in the pelvis area.

- Another key point that I want to emphasize is the **breathing**. Breathing is the most important if our goal is proper belly isolation.

- In the beginning, you may find that you either inhale or exhale on each contraction. That will only shrink your breathing capacity, and you risk to stay without breath or feel even dizzy. Breathing maybe helps until you find the isolation, but do not use it as a technique to make yourself easier in the future.

Belly isolation is one of the easiest from the group of belly isolations. I am sure that you will be able to master it in a short period because it more like a natural contraction.

Exercise. Here is a simple exercise that you can do wherever you can: contract the belly, keep it contracted for 5 seconds and release it. Make as many repetitions as you can. After several attempts, challenge yourself on a tempo mode.

Upper Abs Isolation

We are moving one level up into belly isolations. In this section, we will attempt to isolate one group of belly muscles: the upper abs.

Tip #82 – Sharp exhaling

When I was starting with this isolation, I was feeling that finding and isolating the upper abdominal muscles would take forever. This opinion, once again, has proved to be wrong, and I was able to feel and isolate these muscles with regular practice. It was like a 'Eureka' moment: *a-ha...there you are, upper abs*! It was a fun process, and I still find it amusing and entertaining.

Belly isolation on upper and lower abs means that the belly is separated on two halves, and each half should not affect the other one.

- Put the hands on the upper abs, right underneath the rib cage.

- Feel the muscles in this area.

- Now, inhale through the lungs and make a sharp exhale.

- While exhaling, keep the fingers on the upper belly muscles, softly pressing so you can feel the isolation.

Upper Abs Isolation

1. Make a sharp exhale
and feel the upper abs

In the early phase, you may not be able to isolate these abs with remarkable speed. Practice every day until you feel confident to isolate it without using the hands for support.

Upper belly contraction means that the middle and lower parts are not engaging and not compressing. Same as belly isolation, whenever you work only on the upper abs, you may feel the urge to exhale on each contraction. If that helps you to find the isolation, do it, but only in the beginning. Later try to contract the muscles with a held breath or while talking.

Middle Abs Isolation

Middle abs contraction happens almost imperceptibly.

It results from engaging the side belly muscles. Having contracted properly, these muscles chop the belly on half so that the upper and lower abs are released.

Middle Abs Isolation

Use your hands to feel this group of muscles and to feel where the isolation happens. It may take some time for you to become aware of this isolation, mainly because it is quite disguised.

Lower Abs Isolation

Lower abdominal muscles are also hidden and take time to be separated. It may differ for every person; some find it more challenging to isolate the upper abs, while others, the lower abs. However, both groups require consistency and a permanent upgrade.

Tip #83 – Hipbones line

Stand in the basic belly dance posture and now place the hands on the hipbones.

You will find the muscle that has to be contracted if you draw a line that connects both hipbones.

If you find any struggle to isolate this muscle in the beginning, **sit on a chair** and lift both of the feet from the ground. In the same moment, you will find the lower abs contracting.

Try to get the same contraction while standing. You will notice that when you contract the lower abs, the entire belly gently lifts up.

As I have mentioned many times before, these isolations are very individual and need time to be developed. One thing is for sure – they work. If someone has succeeded before, why couldn't you too?

Roll the Belly

Since we have covered the basic belly muscle isolations, now comes the funniest part – connecting them three into one whole, known as belly roll.

Belly roll (undulation) is a technique that includes contracting and engaging different groups of belly muscles gradually and controlled so that the stomach undulates in different directions.

While you are practicing in front of the **mirror**, this belly motion may appear awkward and unnatural, but in combination with music and costume, it gets a different dimension.

I find belly roll as one of the most challenging, yet the most mesmerizing technique that has to be achieved in belly dancing. It requires much more than just muscle contraction.

It is a manifestation of self-control and self-discipline. Wonder why? To improve the belly roll, you have to control the breathing, control the movements of the rest of your body, follow the music, stay positive, and show the audience that you are enjoying the dance.

In the beginning, you may find it hard to balance the choreography and your sense of enjoyment.

I have been in this trap until I have realized that belly dancing MUST be a time of quality-spent energy. It does not mean that you have to quit following the correct steps, no. It will come more as a relief that you do not have to be perfect all the time, especially not in the beginning. This will give you more space for creativity and improvisation. Yes, belly roll is still a technique that you have to practice daily, and no, do not expect the results to happen overnight.

However, after continuous practice and discipline, when you try the belly roll, you will be surprised at how easily you make this move. You will feel like you were born with this gift, and trust me, you will like it even more.

There are two ways of belly roll: top-to the-bottom and reverse (bottom-to-the-top)

Tip #84 - Top-to the-bottom undulation

Stand in the basic belly dance posture, place one hand on the upper abs, and the other on the middle or lower abs.

Inhale and exhale. Inhale once again and while slowly exhaling, start contracting the upper abs, then contract the middle and at last the lower abs.

Use the hands, one placed on the upper abs under the ribs, and the other just an inch below the belly button so that you can feel the isolation happening.

This connection of the three muscle groups has to be genuine and soft so that the stomach can undulate and create waves.

While you are sucking the upper abs in, the belly part under the navel is loose and rounded like a small balloon.

Tip #85 - Bottom-to-the-top undulation

The second way of belly roll is reverse, starting with the contraction of lower abs and then shifting on the middle and upper abs. During the reverse belly motion, find the 'belly balloon' now lifting in the upper area, under the ribs.

There is a dilemma among dancers: which way of belly roll is easier? I find it more accessible to start with contracting the upper abs. However, this is very individual and no matter which way fits the most for you, you have to work on the other one too.

Tip #86 – Visualize your belly roll movement

How to use visualization to improve belly roll?

What I found very helpful when attaining this goal was the power of **visualization**. I know that it sounds like an old, boring cliché, but visualizing the parts that have to be engaged has eased me the transformation of this movement into reality.

Do not go into extremes that you have to use only the visualization to gain perfect belly roll. No, no. First, make a clear picture of what you want to accomplish, picture the muscles and how they have to appear, and even try to reach the motion in reality.

You can practice belly roll in a standing position, but you can also try working out in a sitting position. This is only for practice, making you feel more confident with the isolations.

Tip #87 – 'Buddha' sitting position

Exercise. Sit in the floor in a 'Buddha' position, place the hands on the crossed knees, and lean just a bit forward with the upper body. In this position, try to make the two types of belly roll.

'Buddha' sitting position

Also, you can try standing on all four on the floor (dog pose) and using the gravity and rolling the belly in different directions.

Review

1. **Isolation** is a term to describe the movement of different body elements separately and isolated from the whole.

2. **Belly isolation** means contracting and releasing the belly while the rest parts (hips and spine) are still.

3. Have your **breathing** under control while performing belly isolation. It is a mistake to exhale on every belly contraction, you risk feeling dizzy and losing breath.

4. Isolate three **groups of muscles**, one from another: upper, middle, and lower abdominal muscles.

5. Use the **hands** for better 'research' in the belly area. Put one hand on the 'upper' part of the stomach, just below the ribs, while the other is on the 'lower' belly part, just below the navel.

6. Use the hands and feel the muscles that squeeze underneath, while you suck in some particular group of belly muscle.

7. **Belly roll** is a connection of the three groups of belly muscle contractions. While the belly rolls, the stomach undulates (feel it waving) in two directions.

8. One type of belly roll is **top-to-the-bottom**, starting with the contraction of upper abs, and

the other one is **bottom-to-the-top**, undulation begins with the engagement of the lower abs.

9. Use the adjustments on the floor for isolating the muscles and for better undulation.

10. Find the way that is most appropriate for you and enjoy the power of this astonishing technique.

Chapter 6: Exploring the stage with belly dance

Why Entering on Stage Moves are Important?

Tip #88 – It is your time to glow!

A saying goes: *You never get a second chance to make a first impression.*

Some may agree…some may disagree. Like everything in life, so it is in belly dancing; there is one thing that you carry throughout all of your performance: **your character**. A belly dancer's choreography distinguishes from one performer to another by the character and the attitude each one brings on stage.

One part of the choreography crucial for making the first impression with the audience is the entrance you have on stage. When entering on stage, you have to show off your beauty, internal and external. You have to enter proudly, full of self-confidence, positivity, and joy.

There are different ways of entering on stage, but in this section, we are not going to explore them. Your entrance depends on the entire choreography, from the music, the pace of the music at the beginning of the song.

There are varieties of movements that you can use. However, those that are full of self-confidence are the best one. No matter what your entering steps are, do not forget to enter with a big smile on your face. Remember, the audience does not know your choreography patterns in advance. The audience is just seeking a fun and mesmerizing performance.

How to Make Chasse to Front & Back (Basic Egyptian)

The basic Egyptian step is one of my favorites in belly dancing. It is very easy to understand, and you can create many variations from it. It can be combined with almost all movements that we have covered by now and opens the space for improvisations and creations.

Belly dance posture. Stand in the basic belly dance posture; feet are underneath the hipbones, knees are softly bent, tailbone pointing down, pelvis tucked in and lower abs engaged, the chest lifted, head lifted, shoulders rolled back down and arms are spread out in a soft low V position.

Basic Egyptian walk consists of three parts: the first one is leg movements, the second one is hip movements, and the third part is arm movements. All of them are performed all at once, creating one beautiful flow.

Let us focus on the **legs** and explore these movements.

- Step forward with the left foot, touch the floor with the toes, and bring the leg back to the neutral position.

- Now, step with the right foot forward, touch the floor with the toes, and release it to neutral.

- When stepping forward with the foot, make sure that your foot is opened outwardly. What does it mean? When you step with the left foot, make sure that the toes point on the left corner forward.

- It applies to the right foot too. Each time the right foot steps out, toes point on the right forward diagonal. Quite simple, right?

Next, we will add **hip** movements each time we make the steps forward.

- Step once again with the left foot in front of you, twist and lift the hip forward. It is like bringing the left hip from 9 o'clock position to 12 o'clock (please refer to the hip twist section if you feel insecure with this step).

- Add the **hip lift** once you have twisted.

- Switch on the right foot and open it to the right diagonal. Twist the hip now from 3 o'clock position to 12 o'clock and add the hip lift.

Having the feet opened is crucial because they determine the direction and the path of the hips.

If the foot is not widely opened out (let's pretend it is pointing straight forward or towards your body), the hip will almost be locked without any freedom to twist. You can try this just to examine the difference. During these leg and hip movements, it is essential to have the knees bent to achieve better isolation.

Now is time for including the **arms**.

Firstly, we will check their motion separately from the leg movements, and later we will combine both of them.

- Straight the left arm forward and turn the palm upwards. The arm has to be parallel to the floor, gently bent in the elbow.

- The right arm is touching the head in the following way: using the base of the hand touch the head about 2 inches (5 cm) above the right ear. Do not touch the head with the entire hand, use the thumb bone instead, just above the wrist.

- Express softness while touching the head; make it teasing and feminine. Try it with the right arm straightening forward and the left one touching the head.

Now is time to combine these super easy movements.

Tip #89 – Stick to the rule

Every time the left leg steps forward, the left arm straightens, and the right is on the head. Every time the right leg stands forward, the right arm straightens forward, and the left one is on the head.

The **rule** is: left arm + left leg and right arm + right leg.

How to Explore the Stage with the Basic Egyptian Walk?

- Stand in the basic belly dance posture and get ready for the Egyptian walk.

- How to get ready? The left arm is lifted forward, the right arm is touching the head, and the left leg is stepping forward, with the foot opened to the left diagonally. Both knees are bent, providing better hip isolation.

- Next, twist the left hip and lift it at the same time.

- Once the left hip has returned into neutral, change the arms so that the right arm straightens and the left is touching the head.

- To walk, do not bring back the left foot next to the right, make a step forward with the right foot instead.

- Repeat these steps several times until you reach at some point in the space in front of you.

*How to move **backward** with the Egyptian walk?*

- During the walk forward, the leg that you have ended up with, and that is now in front of you, goes one-step back.
- The rule with the arms still applies, and now the arm that is touching the head accompanies the leg that goes back.

Basic Egyptian walk (Chasse front-and-back) is very commonly used in belly dancing because of the wide spectrum of possibilities it offers.

It can be combined with the hip shimmy, hip drops, hip twists, and many other variations. It is up to you and your creativity to make an improvisation with the movements that we have worked on before.

Chasse to front & back

1. Step in front and lift hip up

2. Step back and lift front hip up

How to Make Chasse-To-The-Sides

Similar to the previous chasse-front-and-back, chasse-to-the-sides is also one beautiful movement that gives a different dimension to your choreography.

This one can be used with many other variations. Depending on the music pace and rhythm, you can use it in slow or even faster variations.

Belly dance posture. Stand in the basic belly dance posture, keep the feet under the hips, softly bend the knees, tailbone tucked and facing down, lower abs engaged, chest lifted, shoulders rolled back and down, chin lifted, head up and arms are opened and relaxed in a low V position.

- Using the right leg, make one-step on the right side.

- It is essential to step on the ball of the right foot, avoid stepping on flat foot.

- The step has to be medium length, not too wide, nor too short.

- Once you have stepped on the right, the entire body weight has shifted on the right leg as well (ball of the foot). Release back to neutral.

- Feel this weight shifting; it is important for using the hips later on. With the stepping on the side our goal is only to shift the weight on the ball of the feet.

- Apply the same moves on the left leg too.

How to Explore the Stage Using Chasse-To-The-Sides?

This is a traveling step, and we want to explore the stage with it.

Our first direction is stepping **forward**.

- Make the step on the right side, then gather the leg and position it in front of the grounded left leg, making one (middle length) step forward with the right foot.

- Making the step forward is important because we aim to go forward.

- Two most important positions of the **right leg** so far are: 1) stepping on the right side, standing on the ball of the foot and shifting of the body weight; 2) stepping forward in front of the left foot, and even now standing stable on the flat right foot.

- The left foot is now behind the right one, and the left leg is ready for stepping on the left side. You will notice that this movement comes very naturally.

- So, step on the left side, stand on the ball of the left foot and make the transition of the body weight. Oh, yes, this body weight transition has to be performed smoothly and gently, but you already know that.

- Next, move the left leg forward and step in front of the right foot. Your right leg is now prepared and waiting to repeat the cycle over again.

*How to move **backward** with chasse-to-the-sides?*

The reverse walk is following the same pattern. Instead of stepping forward, the leg that has stepped to the side is positioning backward (behind the other leg). This allows you to return to the point from where you have started.

After you completed several repetitions back and forth, we are moving into the second phase of this gorgeous chasse. Are you ready for hip lifts?

*How to add **hip lifts** in chasse-to-the-sides?*

- Using the right leg step on the side, stand on the ball of the right foot, and shift your body weight.

- Notice that as you shift the weight, the right knee is getting bent and gaining strength to push/lift up the right hip.

- The more you shift the weight and bend the knee, the bigger and more emphasized the hip lift is.

- Next, step forward with the right foot and apply the same procedure with the left leg stepping to the left.

This movement with adding the hip lifts is basic; however, there are plenty of variations that can be used instead of hip lifts. For example, add double hip lifts, hip twists, or figure eights. You can play with these variations and find the ones that fit you.

During this walk, the **arms** are softly bent in the low V position.

Chasse-to-the-sides

1. Step forwards

2. Step to the side and lift hip up

3. Step to the side and lift hip up

How to Perform a Camel Walk?

Camel walk is a basic ground for different movements from this group.

I will break down this movement into several steps, which will easily and smoothly help you go through this technique.

Tip #90 - Footwork and body weight shifting

First, focus on the feet. In an ideal situation, the camel walk is performed on the **tiptoes**, but as beginners, try standing on the flat feet so that you can get an idea of the work from each part of the body.

- Place one foot in front of the other (it does not matter which one). The distance between the feet shouldn't be too big, just a normal standing one foot in front of the other.

- Here is the main part: shift your body weight on the front foot and, at the same time, lift up softly the other foot that has released the weight.

- Then drop the lifted foot down on the floor, shift the weight on it, and at the same time, smoothly lift up the front knee and foot.

The point is to have only one foot on the floor in one set and to have the weight shifted only on the foot that is on the floor.

Tip #91 - Knee work

Knees are in a relaxed position all the time.

They are loose and smooth during this body weight transition. Avoid locking, straightening, or extremely bending the knee.

Pay attention to the moments when you lift up each foot. In these moments, knees will be slightly bent even more than before. However, it comes as a natural consequence from your intention to lift the foot from the floor.

Tip #92 - Hip work

We are coming to the most important part: adding the hip work.

Remember, this is only a hip (pelvic) movement, and the upper part of the body is not coming along with the hips. It stays still and centered.

Our hips go straightforward every time we stand on the front leg (shift the weight on the front leg).

Be careful not to lean with the entire body forward, but to bring the hips in front.

You are already guessing, when you step with the back foot on the floor, hips go backward, and the front knee lifts up. I will again underline the importance of moving only the **pelvis**, isolate this part and move it independently from the upper part of the body.

Tip #93 – Adding the hip circle

We are going to add a hip circle to all previous explained steps.

- Imagine that the curve of a circle (wheel) is passing through the belly button, going behind the hips, all the way between the legs, coming up in front of the hips and finishing the circle in the belly button.

- Have this circle in mind, and let's add it to all steps together.

- Stand in the basic belly dance posture and put the left foot in front of the right (it depends on you which leg you prefer to start within this movement).

- Knees are soft, tailbone tucked, chest lifted and stationary, head up and arms are spread all the way out.

Tip #94 – 'The Rocking'

Now begins the rocking part or shifting the weight from one leg to another. Undertake all these steps together, merged and smoothed as much as you can:

1) Step on the left foot and shift the body weight on this leg
2) Bring the hips forward
3) Lift the right foot up of floor/ right knee is softly bent
4) Keep the chest stable

5) As you shift the weight backward, start creating the circle and move the hips from forward position -> a little bit downwards, bring hips backward and you are ready for the new start. Engage with the pelvic area.
6) Shift the weight and stand on the right foot.
7) As you stand on the right foot, lift the front one up (left foot) off the floor and bend the knee that is lifted. Add the hip circle, as described before.
8) Make sure that this cycle is performed very smoothly and slowly.

There is no need to rush these steps. Double-check everything you have to complete and slowly start this challenge.

The camel walk is very feminine and graceful, delicate, and gentle. It gives you a new spectrum of possibilities to explore the stage and makes you grandiose.

Arms Position in Camel Walk

Arms are positioned in a low V position; however, you are allowed to be creative and discover new positions.

Tip #95 - 'Tiptoe' Camel walk

Whenever you feel most comfortable and confident, stand on the tiptoes instead of flat feet. The proper camel walk is performed on the **tiptoes**. Make it your routine in future practice.

The camel walk is an excellent technique for moving on the stage. It is up to your imagination how you will combine it with the rest steps. You can travel forward and backward, to the left, to the right, and diagonally. However, my favorite camel walk is camel walking in circles.

Camel Walk in Circles

Tip #96 – 'The Box'

Imagine that you are in the middle of a box. To create this circle with the camel walk, divide the surface into eight parts/points. Connecting those points and spinning around yourself, you create the circle.

Eight points of the box. In this case, with the box example, our eight points are: left forward diagonal, left side of the box, left backward diagonal, backside of the box, right backward diagonal, right side of the box, right forward diagonal and coming back to the starting point in front of you.

- Start the circle with the left leg and take the direction to the left.

- First, access these eight points without the camel walk a few times to get comfortable while turning around.

- Then open the circle, including the camel walk, and turn towards the first point: left forward diagonal.

- Continue with the camel walk and now turn one-step to the left to face the left side of the box.

- Keep turning the circle all the way on the left until you meet the last, eighth point and return to the starting position.

*How to add the **arms** in Camel walk?*

We can add the arms for even more emphasized movement. In this circular Camel walk, the arm is accompanying the leading leg. In this case, the leading leg is the left one.

Arms are in the position of a basic Egyptian walk. It means one arm is straightened, lifted, and parallel with the floor, while the other one is softly touching the head with the base of the hand.

When you create the circle, use the left arm (leading arm) to open the space in front of you. It feels like gradually exposing yourself to the audience and let the arm leads you to the next point.

* *
* * * * * * * * * * * * * * * *

This circulation around your axis of gravity has to be performed smoothly and softly as if you are almost floating.

Practice moving on your tiptoes and practice, including the camel walk. In the beginning, you may find yourself being **multitasking**, dealing with too many aspects of the body, and it is natural.

You have to embrace the challenge and the obstacles that go with it. After regular practice, you will be surprised by the result you have achieved and will be ready to apply diverse variations on these camel walk movements.

Camel walk / undulation

| 1. Stand on tiptoes | 2. Push both hips forwards | 3. Push hips backwards and bend the knees |

How to Do the Walking Twist?

Now it is time to combine one movement from the hip section with the walking. As a result, we move beautifully on stage, allowing us to use the space superbly.

Do you remember the **hip twist**? It is a horizontal hip isolation where you bring one hip forward while the other is going backward. Practice for a while only the hip twist so that you can get familiar with the movement that follows.

We can use this beautiful hip twist for walking over the stage in different directions. *If you have any doubts about the hip twist, please refer to the section belly dance techniques for the lower part of the body before moving on.*

Belly dance posture. Stand in the basic belly dance posture, keep the feet under the hips, softly bend the knees, tailbone tucked and facing down, lower abs engaged, chest lifted, shoulders rolled back and down, the chin is lifted, head up, and arms opened and relaxed in a low V position.

Try this walking technique on flat feet to get along with the steps, but in an ideal situation, the walking twist is performed on tiptoes.

Let's divide the entire movement into three parts: walking part, walking + twisting, adding the arms. These sequences are of great help in the learning process, and you can come back to each part whenever you feel the need to adjust any posture.

Tip #97 - Walking part

First, we are going to move on the right side, therefore:

- Make a small step with the right leg to the right. While making the step, do not give any direction on the foot; it has to point straight forward and keep its natural direction (like as you usually stand).

- Next, take the left foot off the floor and cross it back, behind the right one.

- Then, once again, step on the right with the right leg and cross the left behind.

- Repeat this several times until you reach some point on the right side in the room.

Now, let's go to the left. The process is almost the same; just shift your starting leg.

- Kick off with the left leg, making a small step with the left foot. Foot keeps its neutral position.

- Cross the right foot behind. Start once again with the left one and cross the right behind, until you reach at some point on the left part of your space.

Make sure that these steps are minimal. The smaller your steps are, the faster you will be able to move.

Tip #98 - Walking + hip twisting

Are you ready to go one level up? Before we continue with the walking, try this simple exercise, which I am sure that will give you a clear picture in your mind of the "ingredients' that consist of this movement.

- Stand in the belly dance posture and lift the right foot off the floor just a few inches, only enough to separate the foot and the floor.

- Having the right leg lifted, turn the right hip backward. This will initiate the left hip to go forward.

- Bend the left knee to isolate the hips even better.

- Practice this for several times and realize that as the foot is lifted, the hip of the same foot goes backward.

- By going backward, the hip 'accumulates' force and strength to twist and push on the next step when the right foot is grounded.

- When your right foot steps on the floor, twist the right hip forward. What happens next?

- The left foot lifts off the floor and goes behind the right one. While left foot crosses and goes backward, the left hip joins the foot and twist backward too.

- Then the cycle continues, and now the right foot has to be lifted and the right hip to be twisted backward.

It happens the same if you go on the **left side**.

- This time you start with lifting the left leg and twisting the left hip backward.

- With all the energy gained, step on the floor with the left foot and push the hip forward as long as the opposite one is going backward.

Pay attention to the following: lifted foot = twisted (same leg) hip backward; grounded foot = pushing (same leg) hip forward.

Remember that the walking hip twist is a **horizontal** movement, so no hip lifts are needed.

In addition, this movement engages the lower part of the body only. Ensure that the upper part is stable, and you are not bouncing in space, up and down.

Whenever you feel most comfortable, **stand on the tiptoes**, and make all of the steps described before. I find it more natural to dance, walking hip twist on tiptoes. It makes easier the transition from one leg to another, and even the hips twist more naturally.

Tip #99 - Adding the arms

There are multiple variations and combinations that you can use with the arms. You can keep the arms in the soft low V position, lift them up, or use them to give direction on your steps.

The position of the arms from the basic Egyptian walk matches well with the walking hip twist. Every time you go on the right side, keep the right arm soft, gentle, and directed towards the position you are heading (right side in this case).

The left arm softly touches the head.

It applies the same when walking in reverse, and your left arm is directing the walk while the left one is resting on the head.

Always practice starting at a slower pace. Do not force yourself to do all at once.

Be patient and soft toward yourself. Divide the movement into several pieces. No matter how difficult this movement might seem (which is not!), separate it into few elements that help you learn it easier.

Walking twist

1. Right hip twists forwards

2. Right hip twists backwards

How to Do Walking Shimmy

Throwback on the Egyptian shimmy...

In the second chapter, you were able to get familiar with the basis of the Egyptian shimmy.

It was mainly a knee work, and the motion was produced by popping the knees forward and backward at full speed. In this type of shimmy, hips are still, and they are not engaged. If there is any hip movement, it is only because of the knees work. Knees are the motor, the engine in this sort of shimmy.

Tip #100 - Hip shimmy

In this section, to make the walking shimmy, we are going to cover one different type of shimmy. This time, instead of the knees, the motion will become a result of the joint work of the hips and the knees.

Walking shimmy will be explained in sequences, which will give us a better insight into this powerful movement.

Hip work

In this part, your focus is only on the hips and their work. We are going to use the technique from the second chapter: **hip lifts**. Please refer to this section if you feel any insecurities.

- Stand in the basic belly dance posture and make sure that the tailbone is pointed down no matter what the rest parts of the body are doing.

- Engage the lower abs, breathe in, and relax the body.

- Stand on flat feet and start lifting up the left hip (tip: imagine that you want to meet the hip with the rib cage).

- As the left hip is up, the right one is down. The same happens in the opposite direction. Right hip up = left hip down.

- Notice that the hips and knees are also being engaged to assist the hips in achieving greater isolation. Oh...and do not forget to have the knees bent...it helps for isolating the pelvis area too.

Set a pace, be present in the moment, and observe the work of the hips and the knees. Whenever you feel comfortable, speed it up. You will be in the state of hip shimmy.

Tip #101 - Walking shimmy

Here comes the most challenging part which is combining the shimmy with the walking. Practice the hip shimmy for a few minutes so that you can get comfortable with it.

Hips are producing the shimmy all the time, no matter what the legs are doing.

- Slowly start lifting the left foot off the floor and make one small step forward.

- You should be very careful about two things:
    1. Avoid any temptation to stop making the shimmy; hips are 'shimming'

constantly, it does not have to be in full speed, make it slow, but **don't stop**;

2. Avoid any exaggerated lifting with the hip from the leg that makes the step forward (in this case, it is left leg). It means that even if you lift the leg from the floor so that you can be able to move, lifting should not reflect on the horizontal line both hips try to maintain.

If you find it hard to make a step with the shimmy, try 'cutting' the step into several parts.

Part no.1

- Keep 'shimming' with the hips and lift only the heel off the floor (in this case, the left foot heel). Your tiptoes are still on the ground. Do not forget to maintain the horizontal line of the shimming hips even if the heel lifts;

Part no.2

- Continue 'shimming' and gently bend the left knee. Stay in this position for a moment;

Part no. 3

- Straighten the left leg forward and step on the floor (flat foot) with the shimming. Even when you step, keep left knee slightly bent.

Part no.4

- The right leg is now behind the left one and is preparing to take a step forward. Repeat the same when bringing this leg forward, most importantly, keep 'shimming.'

- While you make the shimmy with the hips, bring the right leg next to the other and start the cycle over again.

- It is essential to start with slow steps and movements; do not force yourself to pass through the process.

- Another crucial key is the knees. They have to be bent even lower than usual so that you have better hip work and isolation.

It is optional which leg you will use to make the step forward. You can start with the right one instead of the left one if you feel it is most comfortable.

In the beginning, I found it easier to 'shimmy' continuously with the hips on each of these four positions. Whenever I was feeling comfortable at a certain moment, I would shift to the next position. Eventually, I was connecting the four of them into a simultaneous walk. It takes some time to connect these four points, so be gentle towards yourself.

As you can notice, walking shimmy is more demanding than the previous one. It is because you are performing a movement that is more complex – shimmy, and you are combining it with the steps. It took a longer period for me to acquire this walking technique. Nevertheless, once you have gained it, you will fall in love with its power and tenderness.

Arms Position

Arms in walking shimmy can be in lower V position, but I find them more appropriate when palms are close to the hips, barely touching the hips. Elbows are in a sharp position, and they are trying to reach forward. Fingers are also engaged in the basic belly dance finger position.

Be careful with the elbows. Avoid turning them back and close to your body. Instead, open them and point them up and to the front.

Review

1. **Enter on stage** full of confidence, self-esteem, energy, and positivity. Do not be afraid to show your personality, your fulfillment, and your passion for dancing. The audience will appreciate it.

2. **Basic Egyptian walk** (chasse-front-and-back) is a combination of a walk (legs and hips work) and arms movement. The leading leg corresponds with the leading arm, i.e., left leg + left arm and right leg + right arm.

3. **Chasse-side-to-side** is another type of legs and arms combination. This time the step is on the side instead of stepping forward. Arms are mainly in a position of low V.

4. **Camel walk** is a smooth undulation of the lower part of the body. The pelvis and the hips perform most of the work. Imagine a circle going through the belly button, all the way behind, passing between the legs, coming up in front, and ending in the belly button again. It is essential to understand that both hips go forward or backward.

5. **Camel walk in circles** is a gorgeous movement that is performed spinning around one imaginary axis. Divide the space into eight parts/points and, with every step, reach each of these points. Try it first as a simple circulation, and later on add the camel movement.

6. **Walking twist** is a combo of hip twist and walking. The number one thing you should be aware of is: in that little moment when the leg is lifted off the floor, the hip of the lifted leg goes backward. Once the foot has stepped on the floor, the hip of the stepping leg has twisted forward.

7. **Walking shimmy** takes the most time to be improved, so you have to stop forcing yourself to achieve it all at once. The trick with the walking shimmy is to keep the hips moving up and down no matter what the other parts of the body are doing. Hip shimmy doesn't stop when

you lift the leg to make a step or even during the walking itself.

8. You can be very creative when it comes to **adding the arms** on these walking movements. The most important is that arms have to be relaxed and smooth.

9. Not only the arm, **but the entire body also** has to appear relaxed and not tensed. Keep the smile on your face, and enjoy the dance.

Chapter 7: Manage Your Belly Dance Choreography

Do you feel the need to kick off with dancing whenever music starts playing? I do, and it happens a lot.

Dancing is a remedy. It helps reduce stress and increases the 'happiness hormones' in your body, stimulating positive vibes within you. Dancing for yourself is the best gift you can give to your body and soul. It is something personal that drives you into a higher level of consciousness and self-discovering. You discover what your body and mind are capable of. You find out your internal and external beauty.

To me, dancing is something beyond performance. It is a connection with the song, adding my value to it and certainly telling my version of the story.

This chapter will guide you through some basic steps that I find useful whenever I create some choreography. Do not put yourself under pressure that it has to be performed 100% correctly.

Also, do not take the pressure of showing or exposing your choreography to someone. It is all up to you whether you decide to dance for yourself or to share it with the audience. Oh, and the audience is determined all by yourself in this early stage. It can be a member of your family, friends, or even pets.

Tip #102 - Select a song

The process of choosing a song and making a belly dance choreography is not easy at all.

Often, I find it difficult for the reason that there is a bunch of beautiful songs, and it gets tough to select only one. However, depending on your mood and preferences, after several re-hearings, you will be able to decide whether some songs are an excellent match for you.

Middle Eastern music abounds with enormous types of songs.

Here are some tips that will help you in your selection:

1) **Search for a song**. If you already have some preferred singer or group, check from their offer. Otherwise, you can type in your searching browser hints such as belly dancing songs, instrumental belly dancing music, drum music. Once you have some results, it can lead you to even more songs that you can explore. I have found most of the songs that I have fallen in love with in 'suggested for you section' when searching for a particular song.

2) **Shrink the list**. After you have heard several songs, make a top-five list with the songs that you find most enjoyable. Limit this list to three and then make your choice.

3) **Be attentive to the song's flow**. I like it when the song has a flow with a variety of paces when it offers fast and slow moments when plenty of instruments are included, such as violin, drum, or harmonica. This variety of rhythms allows you to apply different

techniques starting from shimmies, walking movements, chest action to slow sections like soft figure 8s, hip circles, or arm movements.

4) **Personalize the song**. Add your personality to the song. Make up some story that you want to tell through the song. If the song has lyrics, it is helpful to understand what is the message. If it is only an instrumental song, it gives more opportunities to improvise.

5) **Visualize yourself dancing**. All the while you listen to some song, visualize how you would cope with it. Visualize which techniques are a good fit for different parts of the song. Simply, make a brief draft choreography in your mind before you bring it to life.

Tip #103 - Take notes

You might be asking how it is possible to take notes of dance choreography. What can be written? Well, there is a lot of information to be sorted and noted.

Use a notebook to write down your ideas of the steps and movements you are willing to incorporate in the choreography.

Take notes about your entrance, such as which steps you are going to use, and how you will perform some parts of the song.

Example: Write down which techniques you are going to use in the first 15 seconds of the song and do it the same for the rest of the song.

Writing down your choreography helps for revising the process whenever you want to look back and insert some changes.

Tip #104 - Define sections

Make sure that you have break down the song at least into four quarters. Check the duration of the song and, if necessary, make sub-sections.

Organize the techniques you want to include in each section, depending on the music pace. Use your creativity and imagination. Do not set any limit to your improvisation, and do not be afraid to fail.

After setting the sections and choosing your belly dancing techniques, start practicing the sections super slow. No matter how fast the pace of the song is, perform each part very **slowly**. This is important for your stability and self-observation.

Defining sections is a great tool for improved memorization of the dancing flow.

Tip #105 - Observe yourself

Even if you are not well-equipped with belly dancing props, one thing is a 'must-have' in your dancing room: a mirror...a big mirror. It is a real struggle to dance and to create choreography on a small size mirror.

Your choreography gets a new dimension when you observe yourself in the mirror. It reflects your stability and coordination. You even get more motivation when you monitor your growth and progress.

When it comes to self-observation, you can go one level up and record your choreography on your phone or another device. It is an entirely different perspective, and it may feel even awkward to watch yourself at the beginning, but you will get along with it.

Recording helps to examine yourself from a distance and more objectively. You will be able to detect any flaws and imperfection that you want to improve. You can benefit from recordings because you can inspect the 'whole YOU.' You will be able to notice even some unconscious reactions or movements that you do.

Tip #106 - Practice, practice, and practice

Having the best notes in your belly dancing notebook will not mean a thing if you are passionate in the choreography.

Keep your motivation on a high level and feel the thrill of your work. Be enthusiastic every time you kick off with the dance. Bring love into the techniques, practice regularly, and the result will be inevitable.

Review

1. **Select a belly dance** song from the endless choice you can find. Select the song that you find most appropriate for you in that moment,

depending on your mood and emotions.

2. Get yourself a notebook and start **taking notes**. Write down all of the ideas, steps, and movements that you want to implement in the dance.

3. **Define sections** in the song and organize the techniques you want to include. Be creative and listen to music to assess what is best for some particular music pace.

4. **Observe** yourself by using a mirror or by recording your choreography on your phone. Self-observation gives you an insight into the 'whole YOU.'

5. **Practice** is the key to success. Practice wherever, and whenever you can. Make improvisations, discover your capabilities, go out of your comfort zone, and cherish your improvements.

6. Add your **spirit** and **character** to the choreography. It is your version of the story, and it worth sharing.

Chapter 8: Summary

Coming to the end of this book, does not mean that your belly dancing journey stops here. It has just begun. Belly dancing is a real self-discovery that enables you to see all of your capabilities. The most important thing you have to keep on mind is to be fulfilled with excitement, joy, happiness, and love whenever you decide to start dancing.

As you have noticed, there are parts in this book that I have been underlining many times because of their great importance. One of them is the belly dance posture. Even if it may seem like it is the most natural part to perform, most of the time, you can get lost out of this position, which might cause you difficulties or pain. As long as you are aware of your posture during any position, you are on the right way to succeed.

Another part is the 'Trick' and 'Tip' section. Imagining yourself in some particular position is crucial for improved understanding and learning. Sometimes maybe it is even the only way to learn. You may have the best instructions on how to put yourself in a specific posture, but if you do not imagine what it feels like, everything goes in vain.

The review section gives you an excellent overview of the most important highlights of each chapter. It provides you with the key points you have to be aware of before moving on to the next chapter. Review section wraps up all skills that you have to work on and improve.

Sometimes, the hardest part is to start with some new challenges in our life. That is why I invite you to take this *Plan of action* and to start with the dance as soon as possible.

Plan of action

1. *Make a belly dancing* **schedule**. Set some days of the week and a time range for your class that will be only for you. It is up to your possibilities, but spending two hours of the week won't ruin your life.
2. *Find yourself a* **space** *to dance.* It may be your room or somewhere outdoor where you feel the most comfortable.
3. *Get a* **mirror**. It is the number one thing for self-observation. It will give an insight into any unconscious movements with your body.
4. *Set small* **goals**. Start with the easiest movements and work slowly. There is no need to rush. Define clear goals for each class and for what you want to achieve.
5. *Have a* **review** *class.* In the beginning, you may want to learn the steps all at once. However, do not forget to stop for a while and repeat all previous movements.
6. **Reward** *yourself.* Life is too short to be rigid, so reward yourself whenever you achieve some new belly dancing obstacle. For example, buy some belly dancing prop.
7. **Educate** *about the Middle East.* Invest time to get-to-know this culture and the beauty hidden

in the music, history, tradition, food, and language.

Belly dancing has brought many changes in my life, positive of course. It is my energy booster, a vital part of my existence, and my releasement.

I hope that I have helped you open a new chapter of your life with this book, a chapter of self-exploration and self-love. Make it a good one.

Review

1. Find time for yourself and make a **schedule** of when your dance classes will start.

2. Start your belly dance journey by setting **small goals.** Once you achieve them, go for more.

3. Do not forget to have a **review** and to repeat everything you have learned from some chapters. Make sure that you have the base for the next movements.

4. Reward yourself every time you overcome some obstacle in the dance. Define your ways of self-motivation.

5. **Educate** and **discover** the Middle East; it is full of surprises!

About the Expert

Aneta Dimoska is a passionate dancer and dedicated learner. Her love for dancing began in the early years of her life. Ever since then, she has nurtured this passion and developed skills in many dances. Her favorites are belly dancing and Latin dancing. She has an affection towards all belly dance styles.

As a graduate of a sociology degree, she is in love with the Middle East culture and tradition. Her interest in this civilization expands through the years following the challenges that these societies are facing. Understanding this unique culture has made her connection with belly dancing even stronger.

HowExpert publishes quick 'how to' guides on all topics from A to Z by everyday experts. Visit HowExpert.com to learn more.

Recommended Resources

- HowExpert.com – Quick 'How To' Guides on All Topics from A to Z by Everyday Experts.
- HowExpert.com/free – Free HowExpert Email Newsletter.
- HowExpert.com/books – HowExpert Books
- HowExpert.com/courses – HowExpert Courses
- HowExpert.com/clothing – HowExpert Clothing
- HowExpert.com/membership – HowExpert Membership Site
- HowExpert.com/affiliates – HowExpert Affiliate Program
- HowExpert.com/writers – Write About Your #1 Passion/Knowledge/Expertise & Become a HowExpert Author.
- HowExpert.com/resources – Additional HowExpert Recommended Resources
- YouTube.com/HowExpert – Subscribe to HowExpert YouTube.
- Instagram.com/HowExpert – Follow HowExpert on Instagram.
- Facebook.com/HowExpert – Follow HowExpert on Facebook.

Printed in Poland
by Amazon Fulfillment
Poland Sp. z o.o., Wrocław